THE AWAKENING

Kate Chopin

AUTHORED by Ellie Campisano
UPDATED AND REVISED by Michelle Rosenberg

COVER DESIGN by Table XI Partners LLC
COVER PHOTO by Olivia Verma and © 2005 GradeSaver, LLC

BOOK DESIGN by Table XI Partners LLC

Published by GradeSaver LLC, www.gradesaver.com

First published in the United States of America by GradeSaver LLC. 2016

GRADESAVER, the GradeSaver logo and the phrase "Getting you the grade since 1999" are registered trademarks of GradeSaver, LLC

ISBN 978-1-60259-805-8

Printed in the United States of America

For other products and additional information please visit http://www.gradesaver.com

Table of Contents

Biography of Kate Chopin (1850–1904)

Published in 1899, *The Awakening* created a scandal because of its portrayal of a strong, unconventional woman involved in an adulterous affair. While Kate Chopin never flouted convention as strongly as did her fictitious heroine, she did exhibit an individuality and strength remarkable for upper-middle-class women of the time.

Born on February 8, 1850, in St. Louis, Katherine O'Flaherty was the daughter of an immigrant Irish father and a French Creole mother. The O'Flahertys were members of the Creole social elite and were fairly well-off. When Kate was very young, her father Thomas O'Flaherty died in a work-related accident. He left behind a family of four generations of women all living in the same house. Kate was very close to her maternal great-grandmother, Madame Charleville, who first introduced her to the world of storytelling. Madame Charleville spoke only French to Kate and told her elaborate, somewhat risqué stories.

Family tragedy surrounded the young Kate. When she was eleven, Madame Charleville died, and her half-brother George was killed while fighting in the Civil War for the Confederate side. Yet, Kate seems not to have completely despaired; she earned a reputation as the "Littlest Rebel" when she tore down a Union flag that had been tied to her front porch by Yankee soldiers. Had Kate not been a young girl at the time, the incident might have resulted in serious consequences, but since she was, her act became famous as a local legend.

While attending a Catholic high school, Kate studied both French and English literature and became an accomplished pianist. She attended numerous social events and became very popular in St. Louis high society. She also became interested in the movement for women's suffrage, although she never became very politically active. When she was nineteen, she married Oscar Chopin, a twenty-five-year-old French-Creole businessman. The couple moved to New Orleans, Louisiana, and later moved to Cloutierville in north central Louisiana.

Kate and Oscar were very happy together and, like the Pontelliers in *The Awakening*, soon became immersed in aristocratic Louisiana society. A gentle man, Oscar tolerated Kate's "unconventional" ways, even though relatives warned him not to. He treated Kate as an intellectual equal and apparently did not mind that she smoked, drank, and behaved as her own person. However, Kate's period of married happiness did not last for long. After giving birth to six children, Kate became a widow in 1883 when her husband died of swamp fever.

Luckily, Oscar Chopin had been a successful businessman, and Kate did not have to worry about feeding her six children. She managed her husband's business for a year but then moved back to St. Louis, only to have her mother die the following year.

During this period of her life, she had one close friend named Dr. Frederick Kolbenheyer. Dr. Kolbenheyer was initially Kate's obstetrician and her mother's neighbor, but he soon came to play a very important role in her life. Because of his influence, Kate began to study science, decided to abandon her Catholicism, and started to write and publish.

In 1890, Kate Chopin wrote *At Fault*, her first novel. She also initially wrote a number of short stories, which were published in various magazines. Among her most famous short stories were "Désirée's Baby," which was published in her 1894 short story collection *Bayou Folk* and which details the fallout of the birth of a child of mixed race, and "The Story of an Hour," which describes the reaction of a woman who learns of her husband's death and dreams of her future independence. In 1897, she published another collection of short fiction, *A Night in Acadie*.

Chopin liked her writing to be spontaneous, and she generally wrote her stories all at once, with little or no revision. She also wrote in the living room, where her six children would constantly interrupt her. Kate also maintained her other interests, such as music; she generally wrote only one or two days a week and spent the other days going to musical or theatrical performances.

Chopin's stories often deal with marriage and present an unconventional perspective on the theme. Her characters face choices between what society expects of them and what they really desire, and they usually decide to follow their own path rather than that of society. In her fiction, Chopin explores the special problems and dilemmas that women face and is unafraid to suggest that sometimes women want sex - or even independence. All of these themes appear in Kate Chopin's second and final novel, *The Awakening*, which she published in 1899. The novel caused a great deal of controversy because of what most critics perceived as her immorality, although the *New York Times Book Review* praised her writing.

After the public uproar over *The Awakening*, Chopin wrote only seven short stories between 1900 and 1904. Her life ended on August 22, 1904, after she suffered a stroke while visiting the St. Louis World's Fair. However, decades after her death, literary critics rediscovered her work and began to celebrate her stories for their strong perspectives on female independence and sexuality.

Teacher Guide - About the Author

Published in 1899, _The Awakening_ created a scandal because of its portrayal of a strong, unconventional woman involved in an adulterous affair. While Kate Chopin never flouted convention as strongly as did her fictitious heroine, she did exhibit an individuality and strength remarkable for even an upper-middle-class woman of the time.

Born on February 8, 1850, in St. Louis, Katherine O'Flaherty was the daughter of an immigrant Irish father and a French Creole mother. The O'Flahertys were members of the Creole social elite and were fairly well-off. When Kate was very young, her father Thomas O'Flaherty died in a work-related accident. He left behind a family of four generations of women all living in the same house. Kate was very close to her maternal great-grandmother, Madame Charleville, who first introduced her to the world of storytelling. Madame Charleville spoke only French to Kate and told her elaborate, somewhat risqué stories.

Family tragedy surrounded the young Kate. When she was eleven, Madame Charleville died, and her half-brother George was killed while fighting in the Civil War for the Confederate side. Yet, Kate seems not to have completely despaired; she earned a reputation as the "Littlest Rebel" when she tore down a Union flag that had been tied to her front porch by Yankee soldiers. Had Kate not been a young girl at the time, the incident might have resulted in serious consequences, but instead, her act became a local legend.

While attending a Catholic high school, Kate studied both French and English literature and became an accomplished pianist. She attended numerous social events and became very popular in St. Louis high society. She also became interested in the movement for women's suffrage although she never became very politically active. When she was nineteen, she married Oscar Chopin, a 25-year-old French-Creole businessman. The couple moved to New Orleans, Louisiana, and later moved to Cloutierville in north central Louisiana.

Kate and Oscar were very happy together and, like the Pontelliers in _The Awakening_, soon became immersed in aristocratic Louisiana society. A gentle man, Oscar tolerated Kate's "unconventional" ways, even though relatives warned him not to. He treated Kate as an intellectual equal and apparently did not mind that she smoked, drank, and generally behaved as her own person. However, Kate's period of married happiness did not last for long. After giving birth to six children, Kate became a widow in 1883 when her husband died of swamp fever.

Luckily, Oscar Chopin had been a successful businessman, and Kate did not have to worry about feeding her six children. She managed her husband's business for a year but then moved back to St. Louis, only to have her mother die the following year. During this period of her life, she had one close friend named Dr. Frederick Kolbenheyer. Dr. Kolbenheyer was initially Kate's obstetrician and her mother's neighbor, but he soon came to play a very important role in her life. Because of his influence, Kate began to study science, decided to abandon her Catholicism, and started to write and publish.

In 1890, Kate Chopin wrote _At Fault_, her first novel. She also initially wrote a number of short stories, which were published in various magazines. Among her most famous short stories were "Désirée's Baby," which was published in her 1894 short story collection _Bayou Folk_ and which details the fallout of the birth of a child of mixed race, and "The Story of an Hour," which describes the reaction of a woman who learns of her husband's death and dreams of her future independence. In 1897, she published another collection of short fiction, _A Night in Acadie_.

Chopin liked her writing to be spontaneous, and she generally wrote her stories all at once, with little or no revision. She also wrote in the living room, where her six children would constantly interrupt her. Kate also maintained her other interests, such as music; she generally wrote only one or two days a week and spent the other days going to musical or theatrical performances.

Chopin's stories often deal with marriage and present an unconventional perspective on the theme. Her characters face choices between what society expects of them and what they really desire, and they usually decide to follow their own path rather than that of society. In her fiction, Chopin explores the special problems and dilemmas that women face and is unafraid to suggest that sometimes women want sex -- or even independence. All of these themes appear in Kate Chopin's second and final novel, _The Awakening_, which she published in 1899. The novel caused a great deal of controversy because of what most critics perceived as her immorality, although the _New York Times Book Review_ praised her writing.

After the public uproar over _The Awakening_, Chopin wrote only seven short stories between 1900 and 1904. Her life ended on August 22, 1904, after she suffered a stroke while visiting the St. Louis World's Fair. However, decades after her death, literary critics rediscovered her work and began to celebrate her stories for their strong perspectives on female independence and sexuality.

Teacher Guide - Study Objectives

If all of the elements of this lesson plan are employed, students will develop the following powers, skills, and understanding:

1. Students will be able to develop a thorough understanding of the elements of Chopin's life that shaped her worldview and her writings.

2. Students will be able to analyze and discuss, both individually and as a class, the important and common themes in Chopin's writing.

3. Students will be able to compare and contrast the different ways that common themes are portrayed in different poems, especially in consideration of the elements in Chopin's life that could impact her worldview (as portrayed through her writings).

4. Students will be able to speak and write insightfully about the important themes in Chopin's stories, demonstrating an ability to make a clear and articulate argument with a thesis and textual evidence, in both verbal discussions and written work.

Teacher Guide - Common Core Standards

1. 11-12

   CCSS.ELA-Literacy.CCRA.R.1--Read closely to determine what the text says explicitly and to make logical inferences from it; cite specific textual evidence when writing or speaking to support conclusions drawn from the text.

2. 11-12

   CCSS.ELA-Literacy.CCRA.R.2--Determine central ideas or themes of a text and analyze their development; summarize the key supporting details and ideas.

3. 11-12

   CCSS.ELA-Literacy.CCRA.R.3--Analyze how and why individuals, events, or ideas develop and interact over the course of a text.

4. 11-12

   CCSS.ELA-Literacy.CCRA.R.4--Interpret words and phrases as they are used in a text, including determining technical, connotative, and figurative meanings, and analyze how specific word choices shape meaning or tone.

5. 11-12

   CCSS.ELA-Literacy.CCRA.R.5--Analyze the structure of texts, including how specific sentences, paragraphs, and larger portions of the text (e.g., a section, chapter, scene, or stanza) relate to each other and the whole.

6. 11-12

   CCSS.ELA-Literacy.CCRA.R.6--Assess how point of view or purpose shapes the content and style of a text.

7. 11-12

   CCSS.ELA-Literacy.CCRA.R.7--Integrate and evaluate content presented in diverse media and formats, including visually and quantitatively, as well as in words.

8. 11-12

CCSS.ELA-Literacy.CCRA.R.8--Delineate and evaluate the argument and specific claims in a text, including the validity of the reasoning as well as the relevance and sufficiency of the evidence.

9. 11-12

CCSS.ELA-Literacy.CCRA.R.9--Analyze how two or more texts address similar themes or topics in order to build knowledge or to compare the approaches the authors take.

10. 11-12

CCSS.ELA-Literacy.CCRA.R.10--Read and comprehend complex literary and informational texts independently and proficiently.

11. 11-12

CCSS.ELA-Literacy.CCRA.W.1--Write arguments to support claims in an analysis of substantive topics or texts using valid reasoning and relevant and sufficient evidence.

12. 11-12

CCSS.ELA-Literacy.CCRA.W.2--Write informative/explanatory texts to examine and convey complex ideas and information clearly and accurately through the effective selection, organization, and analysis of content.

13. 11-12

CCSS.ELA-Literacy.CCRA.W.3--Write narratives to develop real or imagined experiences or events using effective technique, well-chosen details and well-structured event sequences.

14. 11-12

CCSS.ELA-Literacy.CCRA.W.4--Produce clear and coherent writing in which the development, organization, and style are appropriate to task, purpose, and audience.

15. 11-12

CCSS.ELA-Literacy.CCRA.W.5--Develop and strengthen writing as needed by planning, revising, editing, rewriting, or trying a new approach.

16. 11-12

CCSS.ELA-Literacy.CCRA.W.6--Use technology, including the Internet, to produce and publish writing and to interact and collaborate with others.

17. 11-12

   CCSS.ELA-Literacy.CCRA.W.7--Conduct short as well as more sustained research projects based on focused questions, demonstrating understanding of the subject under investigation.

18. 11-12

   CCSS.ELA-Literacy.CCRA.W.8--Gather relevant information from multiple print and digital sources, assess the credibility and accuracy of each source, and integrate the information while avoiding plagiarism.

19. 11-12

   CCSS.ELA-Literacy.CCRA.W.9--Draw evidence from literary or informational texts to support analysis, reflection, and research.

20. 11-12

   CCSS.ELA-Literacy.CCRA.SL.1--Prepare for and participate effectively in a range of conversations and collaborations with diverse partners, building on others' ideas and expressing their own clearly and persuasively.

21. 11-12

   CCSS.ELA-Literacy.CCRA.SL.2--Integrate and evaluate information presented in diverse media and formats, including visually, quantitatively, and orally.

22. 11-12

   CCSS.ELA-Literacy.CCRA.SL.3--Evaluate a speaker's point of view, reasoning, and use of evidence and rhetoric, identifying any fallacious reasoning or exaggerated or distorted evidence.

23. 11-12

   CCSS.ELA-Literacy.CCRA.SL.4--Present information, findings, and supporting evidence such that listeners can follow the line of reasoning and the organization, development, and style are appropriate to task, purpose, and audience.

24. 11-12

   CCSS.ELA-Literacy.CCRA.SL.5--Make strategic use of digital media and visual displays of data to express information and enhance understanding of presentations.

25. 11-12

CCSS.ELA-Literacy.CCRA.SL.6--Adapt speech to a variety of contexts and communicative tasks, demonstrating command of formal English when indicated or appropriate.

26. 11-12

CCSS.ELA-Literacy.CCRA.L.1--Demonstrate command of the conventions of standard English grammar and usage when writing or speaking.

27. 11-12

CCSS.ELA-Literacy.CCRA.L.2--Demonstrate command of the conventions of standard English capitalization, punctuation, and spelling when writing.

28. 11-12

CCSS.ELA-Literacy.CCRA.L.3--Apply knowledge of language to understand how language functions in different contexts, to make effective choices for meaning or style, and to comprehend more fully when reading or listening.

29. 11-12

CCSS.ELA-Literacy.CCRA.L.4--Determine or clarify the meaning of unknown and multiple-meaning words and phrases by using context clues, analyzing meaningful word parts, and consulting general and specialized reference materials, as appropriate.

30. 11-12

CCSS.ELA-Literacy.CCRA.L.5--Demonstrate understanding of figurative language, word relationships, and nuances in word meanings.

Teacher Guide - Introduction to The Awakening

Kate Chopin grew up in a wealthy and influential St. Louis family, and she achieved virtually every milestone expected of women of her class during that era. She got married to a wealthy Creole businessman, Oscar Chopin, and moved with him to New Orleans to become a dutiful and doting wife. During her time there, Kate was part of New Orleans's postbellum Southern aristocracy; until they moved out to a bayou so that Oscar could more closely manage his family's plantations. Kate also became a mother six times over, fulfilling another expectation of women during her time. Sadly, Kate's seemingly happy domestic life did not last long, as Oscar died of swamp fever in 1883, leaving Kate a widow at the young age of 33.

Interestingly, although her writings often portray women who are desperately unhappy and unfulfilled in their roles as wives and mothers, by all accounts, Kate and Oscar were very happy together. Oscar apparently treated Kate as an intellectual equal and did not seem to mind that she smoked, drank, and generally behaved as her own person. It was only after Oscar's death that Kate, at the urging of her family friend Dr. Kolbenheyer, began to more deeply explore her unconventional perspectives about gender through her writing.

Beginning with the 1890 publication of her first novel, *At Fault,* Kate Chopin published her stories and longer works regularly in various magazines. Some of the stories studied in Day 4 and Day 5 of this lesson plan were published during Chopin's life, while others were not published until much later, probably due to their sexually explicit content.

Virtually all of Chopin's writings are set in pre- and post-Civil War New Orleans and the surrounding Louisiana bayou and coastal areas. As a result, Chopin explores a variety of themes that were important in New Orleans and Louisiana culture and society at the time, often advancing ideas and opinions that were controversial. The short stories in this lesson plan are intended to give a wide lens, allowing students to see the full breadth of topics and ideas that Chopin explored in her writing.

Upon its publication in 1899, *The Awakening* immediately inspired tremendous controversy. Kate Chopin's contemporaries were appalled at her portrayal of a woman betraying her duties as a wife and mother to pursue her own sexual and personal desires. Stories like Chopin's do exist at the time, but usually the narrator clearly condemns the actions of woman who is not living up to societal expectations of her. In contrast, Chopin's narrator maintains a non-judgemental, matter-of-fact tone, seeming to have a neutral or even positive opinion of Edna Pontellier's socially rebellious decisions. Due to the novel's scandalous content, Chopin was ostracized after the publication of *The Awakening*, and she died only five years later of a sudden stroke.

The Awakening and, indeed, many of Kate Chopin's stories, were virtually forgotten until the middle of the twentieth century. Today, however, she is regarded as a bold and unconventional thinker ahead of her time. Modern-day literary critics often examine Chopin's works through the lenses of several different literary movements -- the local-color movement, naturalism, and modern-day feminism.

Key Aspects of The Awakening

Tone

In *The Awakening*, Chopin writes in relatively formal, traditional prose which gives a sense of gravity to her characters' feelings and experiences. As a result, the overall tone is matter-of-fact and serious.

Setting

Virtually all of Chopin's writings, including *The Awakening* and all the stories in this lesson plan, are set in the ante- or post-bellum era in New Orleans and the surrounding Louisiana bayou and coastal areas.

Point of view

The Awakening and the other Chopin stories in this lesson plan are all written from the third-person omniscient point of view. This narration further reinforces the somber, serious tone that permeates most of Chopin's writing.

Character development

In most of Chopin's stories, only the main protagonist (almost always a woman) truly develops as a character. However, in a few cases, important additional characters also develop over the course of the story.

- Edna Pontellier (*The Awakening*) -- Edna transforms tremendously over the course of the novel. She begins as a pleasant, if disinterested, wife and mother, although neither of those qualities comes naturally to her. After spending the summer getting to know a young, handsome bachelor named Robert Lebrun at Grand Isle, she begins a process of intellectual, emotional, and sexual awakening that leads her to strive to become entirely her own person, unhindered by her husband, children, or the expectations of society. She moves out of the large Pontellier home into a house of her own, begins having an affair, and starts painting and gambling to make a living. Eventually, however, Edna is unable to feel free except through death, and she commits suicide at the end of the novel.

Biography of Kate Chopin (1850–1904)

- Robert Lebrun (*The Awakening*) -- Edna's most important love interest in the novel, Robert is at first a carefree young bachelor who flirtatiously spends time with different women (usually those who are married or widowed) every summer at Grand Isle. However, with Edna it is different, as he begins to actually have feelings for her. He tries to end their budding romance by leaving for Mexico. But Edna does not stop feeling for him (nor, apparently, he for her), and when he returns to New Orleans, Edna pushes him into a more serious conversation about their relationship. Eventually Robert admits that he loves her, but he decides he cannot be with her because what she truly wants is to be complete free. Over the course of the novel, Robert seems to mature from a jovial, flirtatious young bachelor who does not take any of his dalliances very seriously, to a more earnest and thoughtful man who tries to act in what he genuinely believes to be the most honorable way.
- Madame Ratignolle (*The Awakening*) -- Madame Ratignolle does not develop so much as she has two sides to her, one of which is only revealed at the end of the novel. On the outside and in most areas of her life, Madame Ratignolle is a perfect wife and doting mother, fulfilling every expectation of a woman of her social class at the time. Madame Ratignolle maintains this image throughout virtually every scene in the novel. However, the last time we see her, when she is giving birth, Madame Ratignolle reveals herself to be a person who feels pain, anger, and despair like everyone else.
- Mrs. Baroda ("A Respectable Woman") -- Over the course of the story, Mrs. Baroda changes from being wary of Gouvernail, her husband's old friend, to being attracted to him and conflicted about it, to agreeing to have him return the following summer, saying she had "overcome everything." Although the meaning of this final line has been debated at length among scholars, it is at least clear that Mrs. Baroda has changed in some way. Either her mind has been opened and she plans to explore her attraction to Gouvernail and the sense of sensual freedom he momentarily inspired in her, or she has overcome her desires and now is able to be around Gouvernail without experiencing unpleasant emotions.
- Athénaïse ("Athénaïse") -- Athénaïse begins the story feeling frustrated and trapped in her marriage to Cazeau. She wants to return to being single, not because Cazeau is a bad husband, but because she simply doesn't enjoy being married. However, unlike some of the other female characters in Chopin's stories, Athénaïse does get to experience a semblance of true freedom for a while, living her life independently in a boarding house. However, when she learns she is pregnant, Athénaïse's entire perspective on her marriage and life changes -- she returns joyfully to her husband, and he can tell that it is the first kiss of true passion they've ever shared.
- Louise Mallard ("A Pair of Silk Stockings") -- Louise begins the story as a typical New Orleans high-society wife, when she learns of her husband's sudden death in an accident. She is shocked at first, but as she looks out the window and sees the newly blooming world outside, she realizes that she is now free and begins relishing all the things she can now do as a single

person again. Louise's whole perspective about her life changes when she learns this one piece of news.

- Désirée Aubigny ("Désirée's Baby") -- Désirée transforms from a happy wife and mother, who is thrilled to be married to a prestigious businessman and overjoyed at the birth of her new son. She soon discovers the truth about her son's racial make-up and her husband rejects her, leaving her completely devastated. Although her adoptive mother, Madame Valmondé, still loves her and is happy to take her and her son in, Désirée cannot cope with the new reality of her life. She disappears into the bayou in the middle of the night.
- Armand Aubigny ("Désirée's Baby") -- Armand is Désirée's husband; there are suggestions from the beginning that Armand is an exacting, imperious man who does not keep a happy home. But he does initially seem to love Désirée and their son. As the novel goes on, however, Armand becomes more distant from and cruel towards Désirée, and when she finally understands the truth about her son, Armand is cruel and cold to her, showing no signs of the love he'd once professed for her. Chopin's portrayal of Armand is notably different than many of her other male characters, especially husbands, who are usually kind, gentle, and pleasant, even if they are completely unaware of their wives' true thoughts and desires.
- Mrs. Sommers ("A Pair of Silk Stockings") -- Mrs. Sommers begins the novel as a dutiful wife and mother, excited about the many practical items she can purchase with her unexpected fifteen dollar windfall. However, we learn that, before she became a wife and mother, Mrs. Sommers was used to a more refined way of life. She has since subjugated all of those desires in order to serve her children. When she feels the silk stockings for the first time, however, they draw her in. Mrs. Sommers ends up spending all of her extra money buying new clothing and taking herself out to eat and to the theater. By the end of the story -- now that she has experienced the feeling of true freedom, independence, and pursuing her own desires for once -- she does not want to return back to her family.

None of the characters in "The Storm" go through any apparent character development.

Themes

- **Freedom and Independence** -- Virtually all of Chopin's stories deal with the ways in which different characters, usually the female protagonists, develop their own conceptions of what it would truly mean to be free and independent. Most of the pieces read in this unit -- in particular *The Awakening*, "A Respectable Woman," "Athénaïse," "The Story of an Hour," and "A Pair of Silk Stockings" -- demonstrate the ways in which women during Chopin's time often sacrificed their own freedom and independence when they got married and had children. In all of these stories, the women must choose between fulfilling their duties to their husbands and children and pursuing their own independent desires.

- **Gender and Societal Expectations** -- This theme also arises in virtually all of Chopin's stories and is strongly connected to the theme of freedom and independence. During Chopin's time, women had very specific expectations of them in society -- they would fulfill their duties as wives and mothers, and should always be willing to sacrifice their desires and themselves for their families. Many of Chopin's stories find women re-examining their roles in society and assessing whether or not they actually enjoy their lives as wives and mothers. In addition, Chopin's protagonists often flout accepted cultural norms and societal expectations without receiving reprimand or judgement, suggesting that Chopin herself does not hold these cultural expectations of women in particularly high regard.

- **Class and Race Relations** -- Most of Chopin's stories in this lesson plan are set after the Civil War, when the United States was in the midst of navigating race relations the aftermath of slavery. Some of the tensions among Chopin's characters result from different racial and class expectations. Class and race play important roles in several of the stories in this unit, including "Désirée's Baby," *The Awakening*, and to a more limited extent, "Athénaïse."

- **Love, Sexual Desire, and Sensory Experience** -- Many of the protagonists in Chopin's stories find themselves confronted with sensory experiences that make them think about both love and sexual desire in new ways. While many of the wives in Chopin's stories are fond enough of their families, few feel a deep sense of love and devotion to their husbands. However, when they experience some new relationship or sensory experience (listening to someone's voice, smelling the ocean, observing the lively spring day on the street, etc.), they find themselves opened up to a whole new perspective on life and their desires. These sensual experiences that tap into their physical desires often inspire the protagonists to pursue more freedom, independence, and personal experiences.

- **The Fine Line between Life and Death** -- Several of Chopin's stories, including *The Awakening,* "The Story of an Hour," and "Désirée's Baby" in particular, confront readers with the idea that full freedom only comes through death. Both Edna Pontellier and Désirée Aubigny commit suicide when they realize they will never be able to have the freedom they seek in the world they live in, while Louise Mallard dies of a heart attack when she is overcome by joy. The association that Chopin makes between a truly free life and death suggests that she does not believe there are realistic ways for women during her era to both pursue their true desires and be accepted in traditional society. The alternative Chopin seems to suggest is to attain true freedom through death.

Symbols

- **Birds** -- This symbol appears in several different stories, and is particularly important in *The Awakening*. Birds represent freedom, independence, and a willingness to go against societal expectations.
- **The Sea** -- The sea symbolizes several different things in Chopin's stories. First, the sea represents the depths of the unknown and the full realization of freedom. Second, the sea can represent a kind-of baptismal vessel -- many of Edna's "awakenings" come after she has been in the sea, or has been meditating on it for some time.
- **Cigars** -- Cigars come up time and again in *The Awakening* and a few of Chopin's other stories, as a representation of traditional cultural norms and gender expectations.
- **Serpents** -- The serpent appears as a metaphor several times, always at times when people are about to morally stray in some way or go against societal expectations for their behavior. This symbol represents temptation and human folly.
- **Seasns** -- Spring and Summer, and in fact all the seasons, have important symbolic meanings throughout *The Awakening* and several of Chopin's other stories. Characters actions and feelings are often governed by or, at least, inspired by the seasonal and weather changes they see or experience.

Climax

In *The Awakening* is difficult to determine the true climax of the novel, as there are many points at which Edna Pontellier believes herself to be awakening in some new way and her sense of new knowledge and freedom grows. However, the most important thematic climax of the novel is the scene in Chapter XXXVI, when Robert finally admits his love for Edna and tells her that he's wished for a long time she could be free to run away with him. Edna corrects Robert's suggestion that she would become his possession in some way, explaining that she is now free and can give herself to whomever she wishes, and Robert pales at this comment. What becomes clear in this scene is that now that Edna has achieved her true freedom, even the man who she's been dreaming of all this time is not who or what she wants any longer. This final realization of what it means for Edna to be truly free begins the process that eventually leads to her suicide.

In Chopin's other stories, there are some with clear climaxes and others without. In "A Respectable Woman," the climax arrives during Mrs. Baroda's first real conversation with Gouvernail, when she is tempted to pull him closer. The climax in "Athénaïse" comes when the title character realizes she is pregnant and her entire attitude on her marriage changes. Despite how short they are, "The Story of an Hour" and "A Pair of Silk Stockings" both have climaxes -- in the first story, Louise Mallard begins whispering "free!" to herself, thinking herself to be single and independent again, and in the second story, Mrs. Sommers takes herself to the theater at the end of day of impulsively shopping for herself. The climax of "The Storm" comes when Calixta and Alcée re-kindle their sexual affair during the height of the storm. Finally, the climax in "Désirée's Baby" slowly builds as Désirée feels an impending sense of fear, and final comes to a head when she realizes her son resembles the 1/4-black slave-boy who is fanning him.

Structure

The Awakening is a short novel divided into chapters, while the other stories in this unit are short stories. In virtually all of Chopin's writings, the structure remains relatively consistent:

- the female protagonist seems happy (or, at least, happy enough) in her role as wife and mother, and with her place in society;
- something occurs or new information is revealed that makes her re-think what she actually wants in life;
- the protagonist begins to consider her own independence and freedom in the world;
- the protagonist either overcomes her own desires to return to her previous mindset, or she decides to fully commit to her new desires (at least temporarily) in order to experience true freedom.

Chopin's story "Athénaïse" is somewhat different, as it changes this typical trajectory. In "Athénaïse," the title character begins the story unhappy in her marriage and plotting her escape. Then, once she has left, she learns she is pregnant, transforming her entire perspective on her marriage and life changes, and she joyfully returns to her husband.

Teacher Guide - Relationship to Other Books

- Consider some of Chopin's other novels and writings. A full list of Chopin's works can be found on The Kate Chopin International Society website.
- Consider novels by Chopin's predecessors, contemporaries, and those who were influenced by her. Such authors include Edith Wharton, Wilkie Collins, George Eliot, Henry James, Charlotte Perkins Gilman, Virginia Woolf, Sylvia Plath, and Mark Twain, among many others.
- Read some of the many critical essays and books available about *The Awakening* and Kate Chopin's other works. More information about some of the critical essays available can be found here.

Teacher Guide - Bringing in Technology

<u>Day 1</u>

- *Kate Chopin's Life and Times (ongoing activity)* -- Students will use the internet to conduct research on Chopin's historical, social and cultural context.
- *Timeline Game for Chopin's Life* -- Students will use the internet to conduct research about events in Chopin's life, and may use software or other computer-based tools to create timelines.

<u>Day 2</u>

- *Kate Chopin's Life and Times (ongoing activity)* -- Students will use the internet to conduct research on Chopin's historical, social and cultural context.
- *Exploring Creole Cultural History in New Orleans & Louisiana* -- Students will use the internet to conduct research on French Creole history in the New Orleans region and its cultural and social impacts during Chopin's time. Students may also use tablets to take notes, in place of paper worksheets.

<u>Day 3</u>

- *Kate Chopin's Life and Times (ongoing activity)* -- Students will use the internet to conduct research on Chopin's historical, social and cultural context.
- *Turning Points in "The Awakening"* -- Students may use software or online tools to create timelines in this activity.
- *Inside Edition: Personal Views from "The Awakenining"* -- Computers and access to document-sharing software or web-based services will be useful for the writing and collaboration portions of this activity.

<u>Day 4</u>

- *Kate Chopin's Life and Times (ongoing activity)* -- Students will use the internet to conduct research on Chopin's historical, social and cultural context.
- *Making Creative Representations of Scenes from Kate Chopin's Writings* -- Depending on the creative options available to students, digital painting software, audio recording devices, and other technologies may be useful for this activity.
- *The Woman in Question: Analyzing Themes in Kate Chopin's Private Papers* -- Students may use the internet to look at these papers online, and text-to-speech software to listen to the essays if they are auditory learners.

<u>Day 5</u>

- *Kate Chopin's Life and Times (ongoing activity):* Students will use the internet to conduct research on Chopin's historical, social and cultural context, as well as to prepare their final presentations for the class.
- *Surprise Scene Workshop: Creating Your Own Chopin Scene* -- Computers, video cameras, video editing software, and other devices could be used in this activity.
- *The Critics Debate: For and Against Kate Chopin & Her Writing* -- Students will use the internet to conduct research on critical responses to Kate Chopin & her writings, as well as for the collaborative writing and debate prep portion of the activity.

Teacher Guide - Notes to the Teacher

The Awakening and, indeed, all of Kate Chopin's stories, were written during a time in American history when people of color were considered second-class citizens. Although only a few of these stories deal explicitly with race relations, several of the stories contain casual usage of dated words referring to people of color. It may be a good idea to warn students about this ahead of time, and provide them with some brief historical and cultural background on the time period in which these stories are set.

The thought questions in this lesson plan provide material and ideas that students can use to write short original essays. For the sake of improving the power of expression, teachers should encourage students to write on topics that have been discussed in class, this time in the more formal writing style expected in a literary essay. At the same time, students should not be discouraged from choosing their own topics.

The questions provided for the final paper are most suitable for student essays. Remember that grading an essay should not depend on a simple checklist of required content.

Teacher Guide - Related Links

The Kate Chopin International Society

http://www.katechopin.org/

This site provides links to resources for contextualizing many of Chopin's novels and stories, biographical information, and additional discussions of literary themes and symbols, as well as the cultural and social history related Chopin's writings.

Kate Chopin's "The Awakening": No Choice but Under?

http://edsitement.neh.gov/lesson-plan/kate-chopins-awakening-no-choice-under

This EDSITEment! site (a branch of the National Endowment for the Humanities) provides numerous activities and resources related to Kate Chopin's biography and writings.

Kate Chopin Background

http://www.loyno.edu/%7Ekchopin/

This page, written and maintained by Chopin Scholar Dr. Barbara C. Ewell, provides information about Kate Chopin and the cultural and social influences that impacted her life and writing.

Kate Chopin Literary Criticism

http://www.literaryhistory.com/19thC/Chopin.htm

This site contains biographical information about Kate Chopin, as well as links to images and documents related to her life, and literary criticism about her writing.

Teacher Guide - The Awakening Bibliography

Ellie Campisano, author of Lesson Plan. Completed on July 21, 2016, copyright held by GradeSaver.

Updated and revised by Michelle Rosenberg August 21, 2016. Copyright held by GradeSaver.

Kate Chopin. The Awakening. New York: Dover Publications, Inc., 1993.

http://www.pbs.org/katechopin/

Kate Chopin. "Kate Chopin's Short Stories." The Kate Chopin International Society. 2004. 10 July 2016. <http://www.katechopin.org/short-stories/>.

PBS. "Kate Chopin: A Re-Awakening." PBS. 1998. 14 June 2016. <http://www.pbs.org/katechopin/>.

Harriet J. Bauman. "French Creoles in Louisianan: An American Tale." Yale University. 2016. 10 July 2016. <http://www.yale.edu/ynhti/curriculum/units/1992/2/92.02.02.x.html>.

Day 1 - Reading Assignment, Questions, Vocabulary

Read *The Awakening*, Chapters I-XIII

Common Core Objectives

- CCSS.ELA-Literacy.CCRA.R.1--Read closely to determine what the text says explicitly and to make logical inferences from it; cite specific textual evidence when writing or speaking to support conclusions drawn from the text.

- CCSS.ELA-Literacy.CCRA.R.2--Determine central ideas or themes of a text and analyze their development; summarize the key supporting details and ideas.

- CCSS.ELA-Literacy.CCRA.R.4--Interpret words and phrases as they are used in a text, including determining technical, connotative, and figurative meanings, and analyze how specific word choices shape meaning or tone.

- CCSS.ELA-Literacy.CCRA.R.7--Integrate and evaluate content presented in diverse media and formats, including visually and quantitatively, as well as in words.

- CCSS.ELA-LITERACY.CCRA.W.1--Write arguments to support claims in an analysis of substantive topics or texts using valid reasoning and relevant and sufficient evidence.

- CCSS.ELA-LITERACY.CCRA.W.3--Write narratives to develop real or imagined experiences or events using effective technique, well-chosen details and well-structured event sequences.

- CCSS.ELA-LITERACY.CCRA.W.7--Conduct short as well as more sustained research projects based on focused questions, demonstrating understanding of the subject under investigation.

- CCSS.ELA-LITERACY.CCRA.W.9--Draw evidence from literary or informational texts to support analysis, reflection, and research.

- CCSS.ELA-Literacy.CCRA.SL.1--Prepare for and participate effectively in a range of conversations and collaborations with diverse partners, building on others' ideas and expressing their own clearly and persuasively.

- CCSS.ELA-Literacy.CCRA.L.5--Demonstrate understanding of figurative language, word relationships, and nuances in word meanings.

Note that it is perfectly fine to expand any day's work into two days depending on the characteristics of the class, particularly if the class will engage in all of the suggested classroom exercises and activities and discuss all of the thought questions.

Content Summary for Teachers

"The Awakening," Chapter I

The Awakening starts with Léonce Pontellier trying to read his newspaper on the porch of his summer cottage in Grand Isle, an island near New Orleans. Mr. Pontellier and his wife Edna are renting the cottage from Madame Lebrun, and are therefore spending the summer with others staying at the cottages rented out by the Lebrun family. Edna and Robert Lebrun return from swimming together for much of the afternoon. Robert and Edna try to tell Mr. Pontellier a funny story about their afternoon adventures, but the humor is lost on him.

"The Awakening," Chapter II

Chapter II begins with the narrator's descriptions of Mrs. Pontellier and Robert, both of whom are young, attractive, and enigmatic. The two enjoy spending time together and talking about all sorts of things. Robert tells Edna about his future plans to go to Mexico and make his fortune--which the narrator notes are always imminent but never seem to actually happen--and Edna shares stories with Robert about growing up in Kentucky. The Grand Isle estate where they are both staying has been in the Lebrun family for many years, and Robert has spent virtually all of his summers there since he was a child. Edna tells Robert about her heritage and reads a letter from her sister, the details of which Robert is very interested to hear more about. Edna goes to get ready for dinner and is disappointed that Mr. Pontellier won't be returning from Klein's, a gentleman's club. Robert plays with the Pontellier children.

"The Awakening," Chapter III

After returning from Klein's at 11 p.m., Mr. Pontellier awakens Edna, excited to tell her about his evening. He is discouraged that she shows little interest due to her exhaustion. Mr. Pontellier goes to check on the children and becomes concerned that one of the boys has a fever. He returns to the bedroom to reprimand Edna for her inattention to their children. Once her husband falls asleep, Edna goes to the porch and cries. Although she is not resentful about the scolding, she is overwhelmed with sadness and "an indescribable oppression." However, the next morning, everything is back to normal, and Mr. Pontellier is excited to return to New Orleans. While there, he sends Edna a large box of luxurious treats.

"The Awakening," Chapter IV

Mr. Pontellier reflects on why he was so upset with his wife due to his perceived neglect of their son's fever several days prior. Although Edna's actions are acceptable, there is something about her attitude toward their children that bothers him. From Mr. Pontellier's perspective, the children seem oddly independent, not coming to their mother for comfort and treating their nurse as a bother.

The narrator suggests that Edna is simply not an ideal "mother-woman," one of those "women who idolized their children, worshiped their husbands, and esteemed it as holy privilege to efface themselves as individuals and grow wings as ministering angels." The Pontelliers' neighbor at the Lebrun estate on Grand Isle, Adéle Ratignolle, demonstrates the quintessential feminine nature--obviously and uncomplicatedly beautiful, endlessly doting towards her husband and children, and often pregnant with the next addition to the Ratignolle family.

Later in the chapter, Edna is trying to learn how to sew winter clothes for her children from Madame Ratignolle. Though Robert is present, Edna still becomes bored by this activity quickly. She and Robert get to talking, and Robert lets slip that he thinks that Madame Ratignolle might be pregnant once again. Edna is surprised by Robert's open discussion of intimate matters. She reflects that, in general, her Creole neighbors are much more open and unrestrained in their discussions of intimate and sexual matters, though they all act very chastely in reality. In contrast, Edna often gets uncomfortable with her friends' conversations and books, because they talk and read about these topics frequently.

"The Awakening," Chapter V

Madame Ratignolle continues sewing, while Robert and Edna chat and joke amicably. Every year for over a decade, Robert has devoted his time and attentions to beautiful women at Grand Isle, adoring and doting on her, and the narrator suggests that his relationship with Edna is simply one of these flirtatious friendships (from Robert's perspective, at least). In fact, previously, Madame Ratignolle was one of the objects of Robert's attention and affections. Madame Ratignolle and Robert talk and laugh a bit about his passionate devotion to her in previous years, and Mrs. Pontellier reflects that she is happy that he has not been so intensely ardent in his affections towards her.

Madame Ratignolle is looking particularly striking and beautiful in the twilight, and Mrs. Pontellier decides to sketch her. Robert sits by Edna as she draws, trying to be playfully affectionate with her, but she continually and playfully pushes him away. Once she has completed her drawing, Edna seems to decide she doesn't like it and crumples it up. Her children come up to get sweets from her and then leave shortly thereafter. Madame Ratignolle has a brief spell of faintness, and Mrs. Pontellier and Robert attend to her. After she feels better, though, Edna wonders if the spell may have been a figment of Madame Ratignolle's imagination. Edna watches as Madame

Ratignolle walks back towards her cottage, seeing her children flock to her enthusiastically as she responds affectionately towards them. Robert then talks Edna into taking a dip in the ocean with him.

"The Awakening," Chapter VI

Mrs. Pontellier wonders to herself why she initially told Robert she was too tired to go to the beach, despite wanting to go. The narrator describes a "certain light" that is starting to dawn within Edna that makes her "realize her position in the universe as a human being." Edna is confused by this unfamiliar feeling, but then gets overwhelmed by the seductive sounds of the sea and feels it speaking to her soul.

"The Awakening," Chapter VII

The narrator explains that Mrs. Pontellier has always been reserved, and doesn't share her thoughts and feelings easily with others. However, she has begun to trust and admire Madame Ratignolle, especially because Edna finds Madame Ratignolle's sensuous beauty entrancing. As they walk toward the beach one morning, the narrator compares Edna's subtle, graceful attractiveness to Madame Ratignolle's obvious, traditional beauty, as well as noting differences in their clothing and manner that suggest important differences in their personalities.

As the two sit on the beach during the very hot, sunny, windy day, looking out at the ocean, Edna thinks of a bright, scorching day from her childhood when she was wandering freely through a field. She has the same aimless, meandering feelings looking out at the ocean now as she did that day in the field in Kentucky. Madame Ratignolle takes her hand, and the intimate gesture surprises Edna.

Feeling free to open up, Edna begins to tell Madame Ratignolle about her past friendships and relationships, as well as her current emotional state. Edna shares that, when she was young, she often had crushes on unavailable or unattainable men. She also explains that she married her husband because he loved her tremendously but also because Mr. Pontellier's Catholicism enabled her to rebel against her family by marrying him. Mrs. Pontellier has come to love her husband in an amicable way and also enjoys her children in "an uneven, impulsive way," though she doesn't usually care very much about spending time with them. The narrator notes that, while Edna doesn't share all of this information with Madame Ratignolle, she tells her many of these thoughts and feelings, and this honesty feels "like a first breath of freedom."

As the two women are talking, Robert arrives with their children, and the intimate conversation comes to an end. Shortly after, Madame Ratignolle asks Robert to walk her back to the house, complaining of feeling unwell.

"The Awakening," Chapter VIII

As Robert and Madame Ratignolle walk back to the house, she asks him to stop pursuing and fawning over Mrs. Pontellier. Madame Ratignolle explains that, while she and Robert are from similar cultures and she understands his flirtations are mostly a sort of game, Mrs. Pontellier may take him more seriously and his attentions towards her could be misconstrued. Robert is annoyed by Madame Ratignolle's implication and insists that he should be taken seriously, and they get into a brief argument. Robert then re-directs the conversation to discuss Alcée Arobin, a well-known ladies' man. When they arrive at Madame Ratignolle's cottage, Robert apologizes for his rude reaction to her advice, but still dismisses her concerns. Madame Ratignolle accepts Robert's offer to make her a cup of bouillon before she lies down.

After leaving Madame Ratignolle in her cottage to rest, Robert watches the different people on the beach. He observes two lovers (they will make regular appearances throughout the novel) and decides to pay a visit to his mother at the main house. Madame Lebrun asks after Mrs. Pontellier and then asks Robert to call out the window to his brother, Victor. Victor ignores them both, which annoys Robert and upsets Madame Lebrun. Robert offers to make Victor more respectful and sensible with a beating, and Madame Lebrun laments the loss of her husband, who she seems to believe would have taken care of these difficult, frustrating situations. Madame Lebrun says that it is likely Robert will be able to go to Vera Cruz soon and he becomes very excited. However, as soon as he hears Edna outside, he loses interest in this exciting news and leaves his mother to go find her.

"The Awakening," Chapter IX

A few weeks later, Madame Lebrun organizes fun and festivities for a Saturday night when many husbands, fathers, and their friends are staying at Grand Isle. Many of the children perform for the adults, and then the group decides they'd like to dance, and Madame Ratignolle accompanies them.

After she dances with Mr. Pontellier, Robert, and Monsieur Ratignolle, Edna retreats to the porch to look at the moon. Robert comes out to the porch as well and offers to bring Mademoiselle Reisz, an odd and disagreeable older woman. She asks Edna to tell her what to play and, feeling uncomfortable, Mrs. Pontellier says that Mademoiselle can play whatever she'd like.

Mrs. Pontellier enjoys music and has often liked listening to Madame Ratignolle practice piano. Her playing has often inspired Edna to think of beautiful and evocative images, giving her a sense of longing, hope, despair and, most often, isolation and solitude. While listening to Mademoiselle Reisz play, however, Edna experiences those feelings more powerfully and directly than she has before. Overcome with emotion, Edna begins to cry. After Mademoiselle Reisz finishes playing her last Chopin prelude, she tells Edna that she is the "only one worth playing for." Many others are also feeling emotional and the evening seems to be winding down, but Robert suggests a late-night trip to the beach.

"The Awakening," Chapter X

Once Robert suggests the midnight swim, everyone excitedly agrees to go along. However, rather than leading the way, Robert walks toward the back of the group with the two lovers, while the Ratignolles and the Pontelliers walk toward the front. Edna wonders why Robert has recently seemed less eager to spend time with her, and realizes she misses him.

There are many things to hear, see, smell, and feel on the walk to the beach, all of which give the evening a mysterious and air. After trying to learn all summer, Edna is suddenly able to swim in the ocean, which takes many of the others in her party by surprise. Her miraculous new ability makes Edna feel excited and adventurous, inspiring her to "swim far out, where no woman had swum before." When she looks back towards the shore, she realizes she's swum further than she realized and begins to panic, so she swims back. When she is back on the shore, she tells Mr. Pontellier that she thought she might have died out there, and he reassures her that he'd been watching her. She suddenly decides to leave to return to the house, surprising her companions.

Robert goes after Edna, and when he catches up with her, she explains that she is just suddenly tired and feeling emotional. Robert jokes that perhaps she's been possessed by a spirit and will never again be able to feel normal around her fellow humans. Robert understands how she feels but doesn't know how to express their shared feelings other than giving her his arm.

When they arrive back at the house, Edna wants to sit out on the hammock to wait for Mr. Pontellier. Robert gets her settled in and then joins her on the porch while she waits. Although they don't speak to each other, both feel a strong sense of desire. When Robert hears voices approaching the house, he bids Edna good-night, but she pretends to be asleep and watches him leave without saying anything.

"The Awakening," Chapter XI

When Mr. Pontellier returns from the ocean, he is surprised to find Edna out on the hammock. He asks her to come inside and she refuses, telling him not to wait for her. He becomes angry and orders her to come inside, but she refuses again. She feels emboldened and strong, and realizes that she has never stood up to her husband before.

Shortly after, Mr. Pontellier decides to join Edna on the porch, drinking wine and smoking cigars. After they sit there for a while, Mrs. Edna feels like she is slowly waking from a dream and is suddenly very tired. It is close to morning by the time she gets up from the hammock to go inside.

"The Awakening," Chapter XII

After only a few fitful hours of sleep, Edna gets up early and, without much thought, goes to Robert's house. Only a handful of other people are awake at this hour--the two lovers, the lady in black who keeps an eye on the couple, and Monsieur Farival. Edna summons Robert to join her on a boat ride to visit the Chênière. Robert is pleased by her request and they both join the lovers, the woman in black, and Monsieur Farival on the boat.

Mariequita, a young Spanish girl, is also on the boat, making eyes at Robert and squabbling with the boat's captain. Edna is enjoying herself and keeps looking at Mariquita, whom she finds intriguing. In a language or dialect Ed doesn't know, Mariequita asks Robert about Edna and whether they are sweethearts.

The boat moves swiftly through the water, and Edna feels more free and unhindered than she ever does in her normal life. Robert and Edna talk about other day trips they could do together, imagining finding gold somewhere and sharing it, which makes Robert flush. When they dock, most everyone aboard goes to church, but Mariequita looks reproachfully at Robert as he walks away with Edna.

"The Awakening," Chapter XIII

During the church service, Edna begins to feel unwell, and suddenly decides to leave the service, with Robert following after her. He brings her to Madame Antoine's house nearby to rest. Madame Antoine welcomes them and allows Edna to sleep in her bed until she feels better. While she sleeps, she thinks she hears noises and peoples' voices around her. But when she wakes up, with the sense that she has been sleeping for a long time, it is very quiet and she thinks everyone must have left.

After freshening up, Edna calls for Robert and he tells her that everyone else left hours before, but he wanted to stay behind to make sure she was okay. He reheats food for them to eat and is happy to see that she eats the food enthusiastically. Edna asks if they should return home soon, but Robert convinces her to stay longer and they watch the sunset together. When Madame Antoine returns she tells Robert and Edna wonderful stories about the Chênière island they're visiting. It is dark when they finally get on the boat to return to the Lebrun estate, and again the ocean seems mystical and full of spirits.

Thought Questions (students consider while they read)

1. How does Mr. Pontellier try to demonstrate his investment in and love for Edna? What does her response indicate about the differences in their ways of expressing emotion or love?

2. Do you agree with Mr. Pontellier that his wife, Edna, is not a "mother-woman" (Awakening, IV)? Why or why not?

3. What is the significance of the conversation between Madame Ratignolle and Robert in Chapter VIII regarding his relationship with Edna?

4. In what ways are Mrs. Pontellier and Madame Ratignolle similar to each other, and how are they different? How are these differences significant to the story so far?

5. What is the significance of the events surrounding the midnight swim in the ocean, and Edna and Mr. Pontellier's subsequent "stand-off" over going to bed upon their return to the house?

Vocabulary (in order of appearance)

"A quadroon nurse followed them about with a far-away, meditative air." (Awakening, I)

quadroon:

someone who is 1/4 black by descent--i.e. one of the person's grandparents was black (dated)

"He could see it plainly between the gaunt trunks of the water-oaks and across the stretch of yellow chamomile." (Awakening, I)

gaunt:

haggard, drawn, or lean, often because of age, hunger, or suffering

"His eyes gathered in and reflected the light and languor of the summer day." (Awakening, II)

languor:

lethargy, tiredness, the feeling of inertia, extreme stillness or calm

"They chatted incessantly: about the things around them; their amusing adventure out in the water--it had again assumed its entertaining aspect; about the wind,

the trees, the people who had gone to the Chênière..."
(Awakening, II)

incessantly:

constantly, unceasingly, continually

"He talked in a monotonous, insisitent way."
(Awakening, III)

monotonous:

tedious, dull, boring, tiresome

"The little stinging, buzzing imps succeeded in dispelling
a mood which might have held her there in the darkness
half a night longer." (Awakening, III)

imp:

rascal, devil, troublemaker

In this context, Chopin is referring to some sort of insect that is biting the characters
in the story.

"It was filled with friandises, with luscious and
toothsome bits--the finest of fruits, patés, a rare bottle or
two, delicious syrups, and bonbons in abundance."
(Awakening, III)

toothsome:

luscious, delicious, mouthwatering

"The quadroon nurse was looked upon as a huge encumbrance, only good to button up waists and panties and to brunch and part hair; since it seemed to be a law of society that hair must be parted and brushed." (Awakening, IV)

encumbrance:

impediment, obstacle, burden

"They were women who idolized their children, worshiped their husbands, and esteemed it as a holy privilege to efface themselves as individuals and grow winds as ministering angels." (Awakening, IV)

efface:

erase or eradicate something

"...Mrs. Pontellier also occupied her former position on the upper step, leaning listlessly against the post." (Awakening, IV)

listlessly:

without energy, lethargically, exhaustedly

"They formed a congenial group sitting there that summer afternoon..." (Awakening, V)

congenial:

pleasant, agreeable

"But she died between summers; then Robert posed as an inconsolable, prostrating himself at the feet of Madame Ratignolle for whatever crumbs of sympathy and comfort she might be pleased to vouchesafe." (Awakening, V)

vouchsafe:

graciously (or sometimes condescendingly) give something to someone something that he/she wants

"She did not remonstrate, except again to repulse him quietly but firmly." (Awakening, V)

remonstrate:

complain or protest forcefully

"Children, freshly befurbelowed, were gathering for their games under the oaks." (Awakening, V)

befurbelowed:

decorated with frills, ruffles, or unnecessary ornamentation (dated)

"Her glance wandered from his face away toward the Gulf, whose sonorous murmur reached her like a loving but imperative entreaty." (Awakening, V)

sonorous:

resonant, full, rich

"Margaret was not effusive, she was practical." (Awakening, VII)

effusive:

unrestrained, gushing, overwhelming

"Edna often wondered at one propensity which sometimes had inwardly disturbed her without causing any outward show or manifestation on her part." (Awakening, VII)

propensity:

inclination, tendency (to act in a certain way)

"He fell in love, as men are in the habit of doing, and pressed his suit with an earnestness and an ardor which left nothing to be desired." (Awakening, VI)

ardor:

passion, zeal, intensity

"'But you look tired,' he added, solicitously." (Awakening, VIII)

solicitously:

anxiously, concernedly (sometimes in a desirous way)

"In the lulls, Robert and his mother exchanted bits of desultory conversation." (Awakening, VIII)

desultory:

without enthusiasm, purpose, or plan

"[curtains]...which puffed, floated, and flapped at the capricious will of a stiff breeze that swept up from the Gulf." (Awakening, IX)

capricious:

inconstant, mercurial, temperamental, or fickle in mood or behavior

"There was a sort of effulgence in the east. The moon was coming up, and its mystic shimmer was casting a million lights across the distant, restless water." (Awakening, IX)

effulgent:

radiant, glowing, shining

"But some one, perhaps it was Robert, thought of a bath at that mystic hour and under that mystic moon." (Awakening, IX)

mystic:

otherworldly, spiritual, supernatural

"She was not a supercilious or an over-dainty woman." (Awakening, X)

supercilious:

conceited, arrogant, condescending

"She had a round, sly, piquant face and pretty black eyes." (Awakening, XII)

piquant:

pleasingly stimulating or exciting to the senses or mind

Additional Homework

1. Conduct preliminary research on Kate Chopin's life and write a brief (1-2 page) biographical summary.

2. Following up on Day #1's classroom activity on Chopin's Scenic Language, think about a place, area, or neighborhood you're very familiar with and consider how you would describe it in your own words. Then, write a 1-2 page description of the place, mimicking Chopin's style.

Day 1 - Discussion of Thought Questions

1. How does Mr. Pontellier try to demonstrate his investment in and love for Edna? What does her response indicate about the differences in their ways of expressing emotion or love?

Time:

5-7 minutes

Discussion:

Léonce Pontellier seems to genuinely love his wife, in his own way. The narrator says as much in describing Mr. Pontelleir's thoughts and feelings, and he regularly tries to buy Mrs. Pontellier gifts and do nice things for her to show his affection. However, Edna does not show much appreciation for Léonce's gestures. It's not that she doesn't care for him in return, it's simply that her feelings for him are not that passionate. In fact, the narrator explains in Chapter VII that Edna essentially married Léonce because of the ardor of the affections he expressed towards her during their courtship, and to rebel against her strict family.

Early in the novel, it becomes clear that Edna's passions are kindled most by those who excite her imagination, take pleasure in her mercurial nature, and allow her the freedom to have her own interests and inner life. It also becomes clear that Léonce wants his wife to enjoy a more traditional role as wife and mother, devoted to her husband and eager to sacrifice for her children. These differences lead to many of the events and conflicts later in the novel.

2. Do you agree with Mr. Pontellier that his wife, Edna, is not a "mother-woman" (Awakening, IV)? Why or why not?

Time:

5-7 minutes

Discussion:

Students answers to this question may vary, as students could have different understandings of what is meant by the term "mother-woman." However, it is actually the narrator that suggests that Edna is simply not an ideal "mother-woman," one of those "women who idolized their children, worshiped their husbands, and esteemed it as holy privilege to efface themselves as individuals and grow wings as ministering angels." Although Edna's behavior as a wife and mother is acceptable, there is something about her attitude toward their children that bothers Mr. Pontellier.

In contrast, the Pontellier's neighbor at the Lebrun estate on Grand Isle, Adéle Ratignolle, demonstrates the quintessential feminine nature--obviously and uncomplicatedly beautiful, endlessly doting toward her husband and children, and often pregnant with the next addition to the Ratignolle family. Madame Ratignolle is an ideal "mother-woman," and in comparison, Edna seems emotionally disconnected from her family.

3. What is the significance of the conversation between Madame Ratignolle and Robert in Chapter VIII regarding his relationship with Edna?

Time:

5-7 minutes

Discussion:

As Robert and Madame Ratignolle walk back to the house at the beginning of Chapter VIII, she asks him to stop pursuing and fawning over Edna. Madame Ratignolle explains that, while she and Robert are from similar cultures and she understands his flirtations are mostly for fun, Edna may take him more seriously and his attentions towards her could be misconstrued. Robert is annoyed by Madame Ratignolle's implication and insists that he should be taken seriously, and they get into a brief argument. Robert then re-directs the conversation to discuss Alcée Arobin, a well-known ladies' man. When they arrive at Madame Ratignolle's cottage, Robert apologizes for his rude reaction to her advice, but still dismisses her concerns, and says that he should be warned against taking himself too seriously.

From her conversation with Mrs. Pontellier, Madame Ratignolle can see that Edna feels very deeply and tends to think and act capriciously based on those volatile emotions. Because Robert is so flirtatious with Edna -- as he has been with other married and widowed women in previous summers -- Madame Ratignolle worries that Edna could misinterpret Robert's intentions, which could create unnecessary social drama.

4. In what ways are Mrs. Pontellier and Madame Ratignolle similar to each other, and how are they different? How are these differences significant to the story so far?

Time:

8-10 minutes

Discussion:

Students could answer this question a variety of ways, because there are numerous different scenes, events, and sections of dialogue that demonstrate the similarities and differences between Edna Pontellier and Adèle Ratignolle. Whatever passages students decide to use to support their answers, they should identify and discuss some of the characters' similarities (beauty, social class, life trajectories so far, etc.), as well as some of their differences (investment in family life, desires outside of traditional female roles, ability to act a certain part for social purposes, etc.). Students could also extend this thought question to future days, expanding the character comparison to demonstrate the women's different plot arcs.

5. What is the significance of the events surrounding the midnight swim in the ocean, and Edna and Mr. Pontellier's

subsequent "stand-off" over going to bed upon their return to the house?

Time:

8-10 minutes

Discussion:

In Chapters X-XI, a series of important events take place that fore-shadow later parts of the story and symbolize larger themes in the novel. First, in Chapter X, the guests at the Lebrun estate all decide to go for a late-night swim in the mystical moonlight. After trying to learn all summer, Edna is suddenly able to swim in the ocean, which takes many of the others in her party by surprise. Her miraculous new ability makes Edna feel excited and adventurous, inspiring her to "swim far out, where no woman had swum before." Edna's ocean swim, which turns from daring and thrilling to alarming in just a moment, foreshadows events to come later in the story, as Edna wades ever deeper into the metaphorical "ocean" of personal discovery.

Mr. Pontellier's response to Edna's successful swimming adventure is also telling. She is displeased with his lack of enthusiasm for her and abruptly leaves to go back to the house. Chopin writes this scene as if the two Pontelliers are in a silent stand-off. Edna is not trying to be purposefully contrary, she's just saying how she truly feels for perhaps the first time in her life, rather than just going along with what her husband wants. Mr. Pontellier cannot accept this show of independence, first insisting that she come in and then joining her outside when she refuses. On the one hand, it's nice that he wants to be with her; on the other hand, there are some sinister undertones to his desire to be with her on the porch, as if he has difficulty allowing her time alone to have her thoughts and experiences independently. Furthermore, at the end of the chapter, when Léonce tells Edna that he'll be in in a minute, he seems to be trying to give Edna a little taste of her own medicine and show his will has triumphed over hers in this instance.

Day 1 - Short Answer Evaluation

1. When was "The Awakening" published?

    _____

2. What happened to Kate Chopin after the publishing of "The Awakening"?

    _____

3. Where is "The Awakening" set?

    _____

4. Who represents, in many senses, the socially ideal woman in the novel?

    _____

5. Where are the characters in the novel staying?

    _____

6. How does Edna Pontellier feel about being a wife and mother?

    _____

7. Who is the man with whom Edna Pontellier has an intimate and flirtatious friendship?

    _____

8. Why does Madame Ratignolle ask Robert to tone down his attentions towards Madame Pontellier?

    _____

9. What is Edna suddenly able to do when the group of guests goes out for a midnight swim?

_____

10. Where do Madame Pontellier and Edna go on the boat on a day trip?

_____

Answer Key

1. 1899
2. Chopin was socially ostracized for her socially-inappropriate candor and died only 5 years later, in 1904.
3. On Grand Isle, near New Orleans.
4. Madame Ratignolle or Adèle Ratignolle.
5. The Lebruns own an estate with cottages, which are being rented for the summer by guests like the Pontelliers and the Ratignolles.
6. Edna feels somewhat emotionally disconnected from her husband and children--she loves them, but does not feel an overwhelming desire to be with them most of the time.
7. Robert Lebrun, the son of the woman who rents the cottages to the guests.
8. She believes that Edna takes Robert's flirtations seriously and could misinterpret his intentions.
9. She is able to swim independently and strongly for the first time.
10. They go out to Chênière Caminada and go to church.

Day 1 - Crossword Puzzle

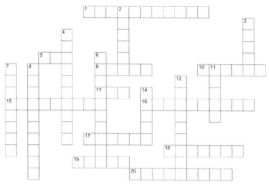

ACROSS

1. Constantly, unceasingly, continually
5. How many children does Mrs. Pontellier have?
9. Madame Ratignolle's first name
10. The bird that appears in Ch. 1 of The Awakening
13. Rascal, devil, troublemaker
15. Luscious, delicious, mouthwatering
16. Kate Chopin's home city
17. The more wild and roguish of the Lebrun brothers
18. Pleasingly stimulating or exciting to the senses or mind
19. The island where the Pontelliers are spending the summer
20. Radiant, glowing, shining

DOWN

2. Erase or eradicate something
3. The instrument Mademoiselle Reisz plays
4. Inclination, tendency (to act in a certain way)
6. The name of the Spanish girl who likes Robert
7. Where Edna Pontellier spent her childhood
8. Tedious, dull, boring, tiresome
11. Passion, zeal, intensity
12. Pleasant, agreeable
14. Kate Chopin's husband

Crossword Puzzle Answer Key

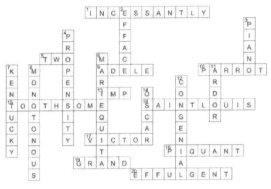

ACROSS

1. Constantly, unceasingly, continually
5. How many children does Mrs. Pontellier have?
9. Madame Ratignolle's first name
10. The bird that appears in Ch. 1 of The Awakening
13. Rascal, devil, troublemaker
15. Luscious, delicious, mouthwatering
16. Kate Chopin's home city
17. The more wild and roguish of the Lebrun brothers
18. Pleasingly stimulating or exciting to the senses or mind
19. The island where the Pontelliers are spending the summer
20. Radiant, glowing, shining

DOWN

2. Erase or eradicate something
3. The instrument Mademoiselle Reisz plays
4. Inclination, tendency (to act in a certain way)
6. The name of the Spanish girl who likes Robert
7. Where Edna Pontellier spent her childhood
8. Tedious, dull, boring, tiresome
11. Passion, zeal, intensity
12. Pleasant, agreeable
14. Kate Chopin's husband

Day 1 - Vocabulary Quiz

Terms

1. _____ quadroon
2. _____ languor
3. _____ gaunt
4. _____ listlessly
5. _____ remonstrate
6. _____ effusive
7. _____ propensity
8. _____ solicitously
9. _____ capricious
10. _____ mystic

Answers

A. haggard, drawn, or lean, often because of age, hunger, or suffering
B. complain or protest forcefully
C. without energy, lethargically, exhaustedly
D. someone who is 1/4 black by descent--i.e. one of the person's grandparents was black (dated)
E. unrestrained, gushing, overwhelming
F. inconstant, mercurial, temperamental, or fickle in mood or behavior
G. anxiously, concernedly (sometimes in a desirous way)
H. lethargy, tiredness, the feeling of inertia, extreme stillness or calm
I. otherworldly, spiritual, supernatural
J. inclination, tendency (to act in a certain way)

Answer Key

1. D quadroon: someone who is 1/4 black by descent--i.e. one of the person's grandparents was black (dated)
2. H languor: lethargy, tiredness, the feeling of inertia, extreme stillness or calm
3. A gaunt: haggard, drawn, or lean, often because of age, hunger, or suffering
4. C listlessly: without energy, lethargically, exhaustedly
5. B remonstrate: complain or protest forcefully
6. E effusive: unrestrained, gushing, overwhelming
7. J propensity: inclination, tendency (to act in a certain way)
8. G solicitously: anxiously, concernedly (sometimes in a desirous way)
9. F capricious: inconstant, mercurial, temperamental, or fickle in mood or behavior
10. I mystic: otherworldly, spiritual, supernatural

Day 1 - Classroom Activities

1. Kate Chopin's Life and Times

Kind of Activity:

Long-term Project

Objective:

Students will be able to conduct research on life during the turn of the 20th century in the area around New Orleans and examine how societal changes may have impacted Chopin's life and writings.

Common Core Standards:

CCSS.ELA-Literacy.CCRA.R.4, CCSS.ELA-Literacy.CCRA.R.5

Time:

20-25 minutes (recurring)

Structure:

In order to understand Kate Chopin's *The Awakening*, as well as her other writings, it is important for students to understand the context in which Chopin wrote, and the ways in which Chopin's world impacted her beliefs and writing style. This recurring group activity will include multiple parts:

- Small group research on topics relating to Chopin's life and times
- Connecting the assigned research topic to the day's readings, and
- Presenting their research to the class in a comprehensive way that covers the full breadth of the assigned topic and the relevant scenes.

For Day #1, introduce the activity and walk the class through the world events and societal developments in the United States (and particularly the region around New Orleans) during Chopin's lifetime that could have impacted her perspectives about important themes in her writing. For example, identify the cultural shifts/themes that took place during the Reconstruction after The Civil War and the changes in women's rights at the beginning of the 20th century. Then identify a textual example of this theme arising in her writing. Next, check for understanding, asking students questions about the observations and inferences made about the selected theme. Then, depending on student understanding, lead students in a guided practice-- identifying another societal or cultural event or aspect of Chopin's life and a textual example of a related theme--or proceed to splitting students into groups.

Have each group select (or assign each group) a theme for the remainder of this project. Themes might include: history of the New Orleans region and "high society" culture in the late 19th and early 20th centuries; cultural expectations of women, marriage, and motherhood in this era; effects of Southern Reconstruction in the region during this period; developments in women's rights during this time period; Chopin's literary & philosophical influences and contemporaries; cultural/religious reactions to the women's rights movement, etc..

Provide biographical sources on Chopin for students to read independently, or have them begin conducting their own research, depending on the time and resources available. These resources could include any of the following, in addition to many others:

New Orleans regional history:

- http://www.history.com/topics/new-orleans
- http://www.neworleansonline.com/neworleans/history/
- http://www.louisianafolklife.org/LT/Articles_Essays/ creole_art_creole_state.html
- http://www.neworleansonline.com/neworleans/multicultural/ multiculturalhistory/french.html
- http://www.museumofthecity.org/project/african-american-culture-in-new- orleans/
- http://www.neworleansonline.com/neworleans/multicultural/ multiculturalhistory/creole.html

Kate Chopin's life and writing:

- http://www.katechopin.org/
- https://americanliterature.com/author/kate-chopin/bio-books-stories
- http://www.pbs.org/katechopin/
- http://archive.vcu.edu/english/engweb/webtexts/hour/katebio.html
- http://docsouth.unc.edu/southlit/chopinawake/bio.html
- http://classiclit.about.com/library/bl-bio/bl-kchopin.htm

The Awakening and Kate Chopin's short stories Analysis:

- http://www.gradesaver.com/the-awakening
- http://www.litcharts.com/lit/the-awakening
- https://jwpblog.files.wordpress.com/2012/01/chopin-study-guide.pdf
- https://muse.jhu.edu/article/31709
- http://www.inquiriesjournal.com/articles/657/kate-chopins-the-awakening- struggle-against-society-and-nature

- http://www.katechopin.org/the-awakening/

Developments in Women's Rights & Societal Role at the turn of the 20th century:

- http://www.gilderlehrman.org/history-by-era/womens-history/essays/women-american-politics-twentieth-century
- http://history.house.gov/Exhibitions-and-Publications/WIC/Historical-Essays/No-Lady/Womens-Rights/
- http://study.com/academy/lesson/feminism-in-the-19th-century-womens-rights-roles-and-limits.html
- https://www.nwhm.org/online-exhibits/progressiveera/suffrage.html
- http://www.enotes.com/topics/feminism/critical-essays/women-early-mid-20th-century-1900-1960
- http://www.loyno.edu/~kchopin/new/women/motherhood.html
- http://www.writereaderteacher.com/2013/06/gender-roles-in-late-1800s-and-early.html
- http://www.gilderlehrman.org/history-by-era/jackson-lincoln/essays/women-and-early-industrial-revolution-united-states

Each small group will then discuss important events related to their group's assigned theme, while the scribe begins to chart the events that could have shaped Chopin's perspectives on that theme. Next, each group will examine the day's readings to find textual examples of the theme. The group will then analyze their selected pieces of textual evidence and add them to their overall analysis.

Students will then share out one preliminary finding from their group with the whole class.

Ideas for Differentiated Instruction:

- Provide texts at a variety of reading levels depending on student ability.
- Provide some groups with the option to read aloud the biographical section, or listen to/watch audio or video pieces about Chopin as a form of research.
- Assign students different roles—scribe, head researcher, lead note-taker, presenter, etc.—based on skills or areas for growth.
- Split students into groups by skill-set or areas of need, so that some groups can work more independently, and the teacher can support other groups more.

Assessment Ideas:

- Student groups each generate a series of charts about an aspect of life or culture in Chopin's time and how it related to her writings, with specific references to *The Awakening* and Chopin's short stories.

- Student groups present findings to the rest of the class, while other students take notes in interactive handouts on each group's presentation.
- Students complete a peer assessment of other group's presentations.

2. Chopin's Scenic Language

Kind of Activity:

Group Discussion

Objective:

Students will be able to closely examine a few selected scenes from "Awakening," focusing on imagery.

Common Core Standards:

CCSS.ELA-Literacy.CCRA.R.2, CCSS.ELA-Literacy.CCRA.R.4, CCSS.ELA-Literacy.CCRA.W.3, CCSS.ELA-Literacy.CCRA.SL.2

Time:

30-35 minutes

Structure:

This activity helps students to look closely at Chopin's imagery, evaluate her in-depth descriptions of people and surroundings, and discuss how she creates the evocative scenes and descriptions of events that she is so well known for.

In small groups, have students find three descriptions from the readings thus far that are particularly good examples of Chopin's descriptive style.

Distribute a worksheet or digital collaborative document with the following set of steps for students to complete (individually or in small groups):

- Find three examples of Chopin's descriptions and imagery in the novel, and note their locations in the text.
- Beneath each example, briefly explain or summarize the imagery used and its significance.
- Choose one example and write or type it out in its entirety.
- Annotate the full example--underline words that are unfamiliar, tricky, or that have multiple layers of meaning. Italicize words or phrases that are

particularly evocative or significant. Write down and evaluate 2-3 literary devices that Chopin uses to create his evocative imagery.

Finally, have student groups present 3-5 of their group's annotations, scene evaluation elements, and take-aways from their discussions to the full class.

Ideas for Differentiated Instruction:

- Give students different media as options for ways to present their ideas, to allow for students with different learning styles to best express what they've learned.
- Use mixed-level groupings, allowing students to play to their different strengths and learn from their peers.
- You may wish to provide the examples of imagery, rather than having students find their own.

Assessment Ideas:

- Students can fill out individual interactive handouts (paper or digital) during the discussion section of the activity, in order to demonstrate their personal understanding of the material.
- The interactive handout can be graded for expression of ideas, support of thesis, and mechanics.
- The group presentation can be graded for completion, participation, acuity of observations, and the thoroughness of its analysis of the scene/chapter section.

3. Timeline Game for Chopin's Life

Kind of Activity:

Group Work

Objective:

Students will be able to conduct brief research about events in Chopin's life and consider how they may have impacted her writing.

Common Core Standards:

CCSS.ELA-Literacy.CCRA.R.6, CCSS.ELA-Literacy.CCRA.R.10

Time:

25-30 minutes

Structure:

Scholars and literary critics have long believed that Chopin's writing was strongly influenced by experiences and events in her life that impacted her worldview and beliefs. In this introductory activity, students will order different events in Chopin's life, first in small groups, then together as a class. Then students will conduct brief research on a specific event or experience in Chopin's life, and write about it (individually or as a group), arguing for how it uniquely impacted Chopin's writing.

Prior to class, select 30 to 40 important events from Chopin's life (e.g. Chopin was born, Chopin marries into a wealthy New Orleans family, Chopin's husband dies and she becomes a widow at 32, etc.) and write them out in order on post-it notes. These key events/experiences can be selected from the Biography of Kate Chopin, and supplemented with any of the following resources on Kate Chopin's life and times:

- The Kate Chopin Society biography of the author
- The Biography.com Webpage about Kate Chopin
- The Encyclopedia Britannica's piece on Kate Chopin
- An Additional Biography of Kate Chopin and her world
- This scholarly examination of Kate Chopin's life and personal influences on her writing
- KateChopin.org--a good source for additional research and information about Chopin

Next, separate the individual events/experiences into random groups of 8-10. Place these groups of slips of paper into envelopes for each group (one envelope per group). In addition, create a large timeline, either on the board or on chart paper, which will fit the full scope of Chopin's life, and allow for students to put the post-it notes/pieces of paper in the appropriate year/date on the timeline. Finally, create an interactive handout where students can place all of the events listed on the big timeline into their own individual versions. Alternatively, use a digital timeline tool like www.dipity.com to streamline the process, perhaps with students each creating their own timeline on a tablet and then working as a class on a larger computer or SMART board.

Split students into small groups (4-5 students each) and distribute the envelopes/tablets and interactive handouts. Have students work as a group to determine the date/time-frame and order of the events in their envelope, then have students come to the large timeline (on the board/chart paper) to place their events at the appropriate point on the timeline.

Next, each group will conduct more in-depth research on one of Chopin's life events or experiences. After they have completed their small group research, students will independently write 2-3 paragraphs about the importance of this event/experience in Chopin's life and writing.

Ideas for Differentiated Instruction:

- Assign students different roles—scribe, head researcher, lead note-taker, presenter, etc.—based on skills or areas for growth.
- Give different groups or students different events/experiences to research and write about, depending on their analysis and research skill level.
- Provide some groups with the option to read aloud the biographical section, or listen to/watch audio or video pieces about Chopin as a form of research.
- Split students into groups by skill-set or areas of need, so that some groups can work more independently, and the teacher can support other groups more.

Assessment Ideas:

- Each student completes a timeline, as well as an individual writing assignment on the importance of their assigned event/experience for research.
- Student groups each generate a chart about their assigned area for further research from Chopin's life events/experiences.
- Students present findings from group charts to the rest of the class.

Day 2 - Reading Assignment, Questions, Vocabulary

Read *The Awakening*, Chapters XIV-XXVI

Common Core Objectives

- CCSS.ELA-Literacy.CCRA.R.1--Read closely to determine what the text says explicitly and to make logical inferences from it; cite specific textual evidence when writing or speaking to support conclusions drawn from the text.

- CCSS.ELA-Literacy.CCRA.R.2--Determine central ideas or themes of a text and analyze their development; summarize the key supporting details and ideas.

- CCSS.ELA-Literacy.CCRA.R.4--Interpret words and phrases as they are used in a text, including determining technical, connotative, and figurative meanings, and analyze how specific word choices shape meaning or tone.

- CCSS.ELA-Literacy.CCRA.W.2--Write informative/explanatory texts to examine and convey complex ideas and information clearly and accurately through the effective selection, organization, and analysis of content.

- CCSS.ELA-Literacy.CCRA.W.3--Write narratives to develop real or imagined experiences or events using effective technique, well-chosen details and well-structured event sequences.

- CCSS.ELA-Literacy.CCRA.SL.2--Integrate and evaluate information presented in diverse media and formats, including visually, quantitatively, and orally.

Note that it is perfectly fine to expand any day's work into two days depending on the characteristics of the class, particularly if the class will engage in all of the suggested classroom exercises and activities and discuss all of the thought questions.

Content Summary for Teachers

"The Awakening," Chapter XIV

When Robert and Edna return from their day trip, Madame Ratignolle tells Edna that her youngest boy, Etienne, has been misbehaving. Edna cuddles with Etienne until he goes to sleep. Edna learns that her husband, Leónce, had been concerned about her and had wanted to get her from the island, but was convinced that Edna just needed rest and would return soon, so Léonce had busied himself with work instead. Madame Ratignolle leaves, and Robert and Edna say their goodbyes. The two note that they have spent the entire day together, and Robert squeezes her hand as he leaves and heads out towards the ocean alone.

Rather than joining the other women, Edna goes to the porch and reflects on the ways that this summer is different than others she's spent at the beach. She realizes she herself has changed in some way, but doesn't yet understand the world of new perspectives and insights that she is on the verge of. The chapter ends with Edna singing a song Robert sang to her earlier that haunts her memory.

"The Awakening," Chapter XV

One evening at dinner, Edna hears that Robert has suddenly decided to go to Mexico and is leaving later that night. When Edna presses him, Robert says he's been planning on going for quite some time. As everyone is discussing Robert's surprising departure, Victor starts to get loud and obnoxious, and quarrels with those who are asking him to quiet down. Looking at Edna alone, Robert explains to the group that he must leave tonight for some business reasons. Some guests begin to loudly talk about Mexico and Mexicans, and Edna soon leaves and begins getting ready for bed.

Edna gets a message from Madame Lebrun requesting that she join them on the porch until Robert leaves. She begins to get dressed, but then changes her mind. Madame Ratignolle comes to see her, asking her again to join them. Edna refuses, saying she doesn't want to change and is feeling unwell. Robert finally comes to see her personally. They have a stilted, impersonal conversation and Edna expresses her upset at his unexpected departure. She had been looking forward to spending time with him back in the city after the summer. Robert reveals that he has had similar thoughts and desires. He begins to explain that these desires prompted him to leave, but quickly stops himself before revealing too much about his feelings. Edna asks him to write, and he vaguely agrees, but Edna wonders about his distant tone.

After Robert's departure, Edna becomes very emotional and realizes how deeply infatuated with Robert she has become. Realizing her true desires, she feels tortured by her present reality.

"The Awakening," Chapter XVI

When Mademoiselle Reisz asks Edna if she misses Robert, Edna launches into a series of thoughts and memories about all of the ways in which her feelings and experiences have changed since he left. Often, she goes to look at Robert's baby pictures in Madame Lebrun's apartment, wanting to understand him better. When Madame Lebrun receives a letter from Robert, Edna reads into every element of the letter, and is jealous that Robert hasn't written to her directly.

Everyone, including Léonce, seems to take for granted that Edna would miss Robert and ask after him. Léonce tells Edna that he'd seen Robert in the city, and she demands to know the details. Indeed, Edna also does not find it strange that she thinks and speaks so much about Robert; she has always had her own private thoughts and feelings that she shares with no one. Edna recalls a conversation she had at one point with Madame Ratignolle, when they discussed sacrifices they would make for their children or others. Edna said that while she would sacrifice her material, mental, and emotional needs -- even her life -- for her children and family, she would never share her innermost self with anyone. Madame Ratignolle did not seem to understand the distinction Edna had been trying to make, saying that "a woman who would give her life for her children could do no more than that."

Coming back to the present, Edna talks about Robert with Mademoiselle Reisz. Mademoiselle tells Edna that, contrary to Edna's assumptions, Victor is Madame Lebrun's favorite son, not Robert. Then she relates a story about a conflict the brother's have over the Spanish girl from the boat, Mariequita. The conversation bothers Edna, though she doesn't fully know why, and she decides to go for a swim. When she gets out of the water, Mademoiselle invites Edna to visit her when they are back in the city.

"The Awakening," Chapter XVII

Back in New Orleans, the Pontelliers live in a stately, tidy, lavishly-decorated house. Mr. Pontellier enjoys wandering about the house, admiring his possessions. The Pontelliers maintain a regimented and structured daily life, accompanied by a busy high-society social calendar (theater, opera, weekly receptions for callers, etc.).

However, when Léonce returns from work one evening and asks Edna about the day's reception, Edna responds that she didn't feel like doing the reception that day and went out instead. Mr. Pontellier is taken aback by his wife's flagrant neglect of her social duties and he reprimands her. He abruptly decides he won't eat his dinner and leaves to go to his club.

Edna reflects that she would have been very troubled and shamed by such an argument in the past, but now she felt an "inward fire" and a sense of stubborn deliberation. She finishes her dinner and goes to her room. Soon, upsetting and frustrating voices overcome Edna. Edna begins to shred a handkerchief, angrily throws and stomps on her wedding ring, and breaks a vase. The maid comes in to check on her after hearing the vase break and, as she picks up the shards, she gives Edna her wedding ring back. Edna slips it back on her finger.

"The Awakening," Chapter XVIII

The following day, Mr. Pontellier wants Edna to come with him to pick out new fixtures for the library. Edna argues that they don't need new fixtures, and they get into an brief argument about spending and money. Kissing her goodbye, Mr.

Pontellier notes that she looks unwell and tells her to take care of herself. Feeling weak and ill, Edna feels dazed and eventually goes inside.

Edna looks over some of her favorite sketches and drawings, and then decides to take them over to Madame Ratignolle's for feedback. As she walks, she thinks obsessively about Robert. She's happy to have maintained a friendship with the Ratignolles, as she loves their quaint, French home. Madame Ratignolle, as radiant and beautiful as ever, finishes her tidying and examines some of Edna's sketches. Madame graciously and extensively praises Edna's artistry. Edna is flattered, although she knows Madame is exaggerating her skill. Nevertheless, Edna feels more confident about her ability and the possibility that she could study art more seriously.

Edna gives some sketches to Madame Ratignolle as a gift, and stays to have dinner with the couple. She notes how perfectly suited the Ratignolles are for each other, and how well Madame listens to everything her husband says. After leaving the Ratignolles, Edna feels saddened because she thinks Madame Ratignolle is missing out on the world by living the life she's chosen.

"The Awakening," Chapter XIX

Edna begins to feel that it was "very foolish, very childish" to have the kind of outburst she did a few days before. Instead, she decides to simply follow her desires without asking for permission or apologizing. She chooses to stop holding receptions for callers on Tuesday afternoons, and generally shirks the social responsibilities expected of women of the Pontellier's class. Instead, she paints all day and basically does whatever she wants with her time. Mr. Pontellier becomes aggravated at his wife and wants to know what's happening to her. Edna dismissively tells him that she just wants to paint and that he should leave her alone; he does so, but wonders if she might be mentally unstable.

Mr. Pontellier does let his wife do what she wishes for a while. Edna has her sons, the nurse, and the maid pose for her paintings. As she paints, Edna periodically sings, "Ah! si tu savais!" (the song that Robert used to sing), and she is reminded of her summer by the sea and longs to see Robert. Edna experiences vast and rapid mood swings without apparent reason or warning -- some days she feels vibrant and energetic, and others she feels profoundly depressed and nihilistic, and thinks that life is meaningless.

"The Awakening," Chapter XX

One day when Edna is in one of her depressive moods, Edna decides to call on Mademoiselle Reisz. However, when she arrives at the apartment, new occupants live there and none of the neighbors know Mademoiselle's new address. Edna decides to call on Madame Lebrun to ask after Mademoiselle Reisz. From the outside, the Lebrun house is very stately and prison-like, with high fences and bars on many of the windows. Edna rings the bell and Victor answers, seeming happy to

Day 2 - Reading Assignment, Questions, Vocabulary

see her. Victor lashes out at a black servant and tells her to get Madame Lebrun, and then Victor and Edna sit on the porch to wait. Victor tells her that he's just yesterday arrived back in the city from Grand Isle, on the pretense of doing business, but in fact to have some fun. Madame Lebrun's entrance interrupts Victor's risqué tale about a flirty girl.

The picture of hospitality, Madame Lebrun chats with Edna and notes how tiresome the city is since everyone is working so much of the time. Victor reads Edna two of Robert's letters from Mexico and Edna is depressed that he does not mention her.

Before leaving, Edna asks for Mademoiselle Reisz's new address. After she leaves, Victor and Madame Lebrun remark on how "ravishing" Edna looks, commenting that "the city atmosphere has improved her. Some way she doesn't seem like the same woman."

"The Awakening," Chapter XXI

Edna goes to Mademoiselle Reisz's apartment, which is smaller and shabbier than she'd expected. Mademoiselle Reisz is surprised and delighted to see Edna -- she hadn't expected someone of Edna's high social status to actually visit her. The two women chat candidly and have a mid-day snack. Then, Mademoiselle Reisz mentions that Robert wrote her a letter, and that it is full of mentions of Edna. Edna repeatedly demands to see the letter and Mademoiselle continually refuses. Finally, they change the subject, and Edna tells Mademoiselle Reisz that she is trying to become a serious painter. Mademoiselle tells Edna honestly that she doesn't know if Edna has the "courageous soul" needed to become a true artist.

In a playful attempt to demonstrate her "persistence," Edna redoubles her efforts to see Robert's letter and also asks Mademoiselle Reisz to play the Chopin Impromptu. Mademoiselle gives in and lets Edna read Robert's letter as she improvises on the piano, eventually playing Chopin's Impromptu. Edna continues to read and listen to Mademoiselle Reisz's beautiful, haunting piano playing as the the light fades and the day turns into evening. Edna becomes overwhelmed, sobbing as she did one midnight at Grand Isle when she was overcome by new emotions she'd never experienced before. Still crying, Edna leaves Mademoiselle Reisz's flat, asking if she can return. After her departure, Mademoiselle looks at Robert's letter and notices that it is "crumpled and damp with tears."

"The Awakening," Chapter XXII

On his way to work one day, Mr. Pontellier stops by the office of the family doctor, Doctor Mandelet, to consult him about Edna's odd behavior and changes in mood. Léonce describes his wife's symptoms: letting the housework go, picking fights with him, choosing not to sleep with him, and talking about "eternal rights of women." The Doctor asks if Edna has been spending time with "pseudo-intellectual women." He also asks about any family history of mental instability, and Mr. Pontellier tells him about Edna's (relatively normal) family and mentions that her youngest sister is getting married shortly. When the Doctor suggests Edna go to the wedding to spend some time "among her own people," Mr. Pontellier fumes that Edna refuses to attend, having told him that "a wedding is one of the most lamentable spectacles on earth."

The Doctor suggests Mr. Pontellier not bother his wife for a while and try not to let her odd behavior and moods bother him. He argues that women are mysterious and complex, and men can't possibly decipher their enigmatic ways. The Doctor says he can come by to check in on her himself later in the week. Before leaving, Mr. Pontellier tells the Doctor that he has business in New York that could keep him there for some time. The Doctor suggests that Mr. Pontellier bring Edna along if she'll go, and also cautions him that it may take three months or more for Edna to regain her usual temperament and behavior, but not to worry. After Mr. Pontellier's departure, the Doctor considers what man might be causing Edna to act so unusually, but "knew his Creole too well to make such a blunder" as bringing this thought up to Léonce.

"The Awakening," Chapter XXIII

Edna's father comes to visit, and she is very glad to have him there, although mostly because she wants someone or something new on which to focus her emotional energy. She knows she will tire of him soon enough, but dotes on him in the meantime to occupy and entertain herself. Mr. Pontellier assists Edna's father in the two purposes for his visit: buying a wedding gift and a new suit for her younger sister's approaching wedding. Edna's father is a former Confederate colonel and takes pride in his distinguished appearance and background. The Colonel enjoys posing as Edna paints him, and generally conducts himself in a serious, solemn manner, while drinking toddies and mixed cocktails throughout the day.

Edna takes her father to a soirée musicale at the Ratignolles' home, and the couple treats the Colonel as an honored and respected guest. Edna is amazed by Madame Ratignolle's ability to charm and flirt with her father. Edna has almost no idea how to do what Madame Ratignolle does so naturally; instead, she just chats with a few men she finds intriguing or attractive. Mr. Pontellier goes to his club on his own rather than attending the soirée musicale with his wife and the Colonel, because he thinks such events are "bourgeois." Madame Ratignolle expresses concern that Mr. Pontellier does not stay home and spend time with his wife more often; Edna replies that if he were there, they "wouldn't have anything to say to each other."

As promised, Doctor Mandelet calls on Edna. Edna has just returned from racetrack, and seemed lively and happy. She and her father had a fun, sociable, and profitable day, and were in high spirits. Mr. Pontellier, knowing of his father-in-law's past gambling problems, notes his disapproval of their racetrack betting, and they all squabble briefly about the issue. The group then moves on to telling stories. The Doctor tells one about an unfaithful woman that elicits no significant reaction from Mrs. Pontellier. Edna responds with a vividly descriptive story about how a woman runs away on a boat with her lover one night. After dinner, the Doctor leaves the

Pontelliers' house having observed Edna's manner, affect, and behavior all evening. The Doctor sees that she looks as vibrant, young, and happy as he's ever seen her, and he is sad to have discovered what he believes to be her secret. He says aloud that he hopes the other man is not Alcée Arobin (the noted philanderer).

"The Awakening," Chapter XXIV

Just before the Colonel leaves, he and Edna have an argument over her refusal to attend her sister's wedding. Mr. Pontellier doesn't contradict his wife or intervene; but as her father is leaving, Léonce agrees to attend the wedding on the way to New York and bring many luxurious gifts to make up for his wife's social indiscretions. The Colonel suggests that Mr. Pontellier should be more strict with Edna and make his wife do her duties. Léonce doesn't respond, but considers how the Colonel "coerced his own wife into her grave."

Edna is glad to see her father leave, but surprisingly sad about her husband's imminent departure. She is suddenly very affectionate and doting towards Léonce, acting like an ideal wife for the brief time before he leaves for New York. Her sons also leave to spend time at their Grandmother Pontellier's house in the country. After everyone leaves, Edna feels a "radiant peace." She walks around the house and gardens, feeling like she's seeing everything for the first time. The cook prepares her a tasty quiet dinner for Edna to have alone, as she requested. Edna briefly thinks about her husband and children and then goes to read in the library. She realizes she'd like to read more, and resolves to do so. Edna goes to bed feeling a sense of calm and peace she hadn't previously known.

"The Awakening," Chapter XXV

Edna and Alcée Arobin's friendship begins to develop in this chapter. Edna's moods fluctuate frequently between excitement about the future and despair over experiences passing her by. She starts going to the racetrack a lot, attending once with Mrs. Highcamp and Alcée Arobin. Edna is good at betting on the races, especially that day, and others in the audience notice her excitement, enthusiasm, and good luck. They all dine together afterwards, which turns out to be rather boring.

Arobin escorts Edna home and, after he leaves, Edna feels restless and awake. She has a snack and thinks about how she wants something to happen in her life, to do something to shake things up a bit. She counts the money she'd won that day and then, not knowing what else to do, goes to bed. She awakes in the middle of the night, realizing that she'd forgotten to write her daily letter to Mr. Pontellier.

A few days later, Arobin and Edna end up going to the races together alone. Arobin stays for dinner and he and Edna have a lively conversation in which he shows her his sword scar. Edna accidentally touches Arobin's hand and, impulsively, squeezes it. Embarrassed, she pulls away immediately, and Arobin pursues her. He asks her to go to the races again and to see her paintings, but she refuses, saying that she doesn't like him. Arobin kisses her hand and tries to make amends and woo her; Edna responds that she must have misled him accidentally. He says that she has simply drawn him in without meaning to do so, but that he will go away if she wishes it. After Arobin departs, she feels shame about being unfaithful, not to her husband, but to Robert. Yet, as Edna is trying to go to sleep, she remembers the feeling of Arobin's lips on her hand and it lulls her to sleep.

"The Awakening," Chapter XXVI

In a note, Arobin apologizes to Edna for his impropriety. She responds in a friendly, nonchalant manner, and he starts calling on her daily. Arobin acts adoringly towards her, and Edna enjoys his easy company and often feels physical desire for him.

One rainy day, Edna pays her regular visit to Mademoiselle Reisz. Edna tells Mademoiselle that she plans to move out of the large Pontellier house into a smaller one close-by. Initially, she claims that her current home is just too big for her to live in alone, but then she reveals that her true motive is to attain freedom and independence from her husband. Edna believes she can support her own household with money earned from gambling at the racetrack and selling her artwork. By the time Léonce returns from New York, she hopes to be entirely self-sufficient, so that she will "never again...belong to another than herself." Edna excitedly tells Mademoiselle about a big party she will have before she leaves the Pontellier home.

The women's conversation then turns to another letter Mademoiselle Reisz has received from Robert. Mademoiselle tells Edna that Robert does not know she sees the letters, and reveals that Robert does not write to Edna directly because he is in love with her. Mademoiselle Reisz plays the piano as Edna pores over Robert's letter. Edna is overwhelmed with excitement when she reads that Robert is returning to New Orleans soon. Mademoiselle Reisz asks Edna seriously if she loves Robert too and, for the first time, Edna admits her true feelings. When Mademoiselle asks Edna to explain her feelings, she cannot -- she just knows she is in love with Robert. Joyous at the news she's learned, Edna leaves Mademoiselle Reisz's home, and decides to send candy to her children and a friendly letter to Mr. Pontellier.

Thought Questions (students consider while they read)

1. What do you think bothers Edna about the conversation she has with Mademoiselle Reisz regarding Robert in Chapter XVI?

2. Why do you think Mrs. Pontellier pursues a friendship with Mademoiselle Reisz?

3. What do you think of the advice that Doctor Mandelet gives Mr. Pontellier about his wife? Would you tell Mr. Pontellier something different?

4. In Chapter XXII, after the Doctor's conversation with Mr. Pontellier, Chopin writes: "The Doctor would have liked during the course of the conversation to ask, 'Is there any man in the case?' but he knew his Creole too well to make such a blunder as that." What do you think this line means? How does it reflect the New Orleans high society social norms and conventions examined in the novel?

5. What do you the significance is of Edna's final thoughts related to her family in Chapter XXVI? How might these thoughts be related to her feelings for and exciting news about Robert? How might the thoughts be connected to her plans for her future as a self-sufficient artist?

Vocabulary (in order of appearance)

"Edna took him in her arms, and seating herself in the rocker, began to coddle and caress him, calling him all manner of tender names, soothing him to sleep." (Awakening, XIV)

coddle:

pamper, fawn over

"No one would listen to him but old Monsieur Farival, who went into convulsions over the droll story." (Awakening, XV)

droll:

funny or comical in an unusual or peculiar manner

"She changed her gown for a more comfortable and commodious wrapper." (Awakening, XV)

commodious:

spacious, roomy, comfortable

"She started to dress again, and got as far advanced as to remove her peignoir." (Awakening, XV)

peignoir:

a light nightgown or dressing gown for a woman

"Edna bit her handkerchief convulsively, striving to hold back and to hide..." (Awakening, XV)

convulsively:

spasmodically; with sudden, violent movements

"For the first time she recognized anew the symptoms of infatuation which she had felt incipiently as a child, as a girl in her earliest teens, and later as a young woman." (Awakening, XV)

incipiently:

with a sense of just awakening, dawning, or emerging

"It did not strike her as in the least grotesque that she should be making of Robert the object of conversation..." (Awakening, XVI)

grotesque:

twisted, distorted, bizarre (sometimes comically so)

"A light-colored mulatto boy, in dress coat and bearing a diminutive silver tray for the reception of cards, admitted them." (Awakening, XVII)

mulatto:

someone who is of mixed black and white ethnic descent, usually one black and one white parent

"'Out!' exclaimed her husband, with something like genuine consternation in his voice..." (Awakening, XVII)

consternation:

dismay, great concern, anxiety

"'I'm not making any fuss over it. But it's just such seeming trifles that we've got to take seriously; such things count." (Awakening, XVII)

trifle:

something that is trivial or unimportant

"A maid, alarmed at the din of breaking glass, entered the room to discover what was the matter." (Awakening, XVII)

din:

loud, alarming or unpleasant sound

"...though it did not take [Edna] long to discover that was no dinner of herbs, but a delicious repast, simple, choice, and in every way satisfying." (Awakening, XVIII)

repast:

meal or feast

"Monsieur Ratignolle was delighted to see her, though he found her looking not so well as at Grand Isle, and he advised a tonic." (Awakening, XVIII)

tonic:

a restorative medicinal drink

"It was not a condition of life which fitted her, and she could see in it but an appalling and hopeless ennui." (Awakening, XVIII)

ennui:

a sense of dissatisfaction, tedium, or listlessness, due to being understimulated

"...in which no moment of anguish ever visited her soul, in which she would never have the taste of life's delirium." (Awakening, XVIII)

delirium:

insanity, madness, intoxicated or delusional disturbance

"She was visited by no more outbursts, moving her to such futile expedients..." (Awakening, XVIII)

expedient:

means, method, tactic

"Before she saw them Edna could hear the altercation..." (Awakening, XX)

altercation:

argument, fight, quarrel

"He was a dark-browed, good-looking youngster of nineteen, greatly resembling his mother, but with ten times her impetuosity." (Awakening, XX)

impetuosity:

the quality of being impulsive, capricious, or rash

"He wouldn't want his mother to know, and he began to talk in a whisper. He was scintillant with recollections." (Awakening, XX)

scintillant:

full of something excitingly clever, skillful, or dazzling

"The despondent frame of mind in which she had left home began again to overtake her..." (Awakening, XX)

despondent:

depressed, dispirited, downcast

"She seemed strikingly homely standing there in the afternoon light." (Awakening, XXI)

homely:

plain or unattractive in appearance

"'I don't know whether I like you or not,' replied Edna, gazing down at the little woman with a quizzical look." (Awakening XXI)

quizzical:

curious, puzzled (sometimes in an amused way)

"He stared up disapprovingly over his eye-glasses as Mr. Pontellier entered, wondering who had the temerity to disturb him at that hour of the morning." (Awakening, XXII)

temerity:

audacity, nerve, boldness

"Edna marveled, not comprehending. She herself was almost devoid of coquetry." (Awakening, XXIII)

coquetry:

flirtatious manner or behavior

"Her husband noticed, and thought it was the expression of a deep filial attachment which he had never suspected." (Awakening, XXIII)

filial:

dutiful manner, affection or devotion typical of a daughter or son

Additional Homework

1. Using the information learned in the Who Are You, Really?: Character Development in "The Awakening" classroom activity, complete an individual 1-page character profile (e.g. Facebook-type profile) or character analysis for a character of your choice from the novel.

Day 2 - Discussion of Thought Questions

1. What do you think bothers Edna about the conversation she has with Mademoiselle Reisz regarding Robert in Chapter XVI?

Time:

5-7 minutes

Discussion:

Student answers to this question could vary widely and it could expand to a larger discussion of Edna's lack of understanding of her own feelings. Mademoiselle Reisz asks Edna if she misses Robert, which launches Edna into a series of thoughts and memories about all of the ways in which her feelings and experiences have changed since he left. Then, coming back to the present, Edna talks about Robert with Mademoiselle Reisz. The conversation bothers Edna, though she doesn't fully know why, and she decides to go for a swim.

Edna is likely bothered because she is jealous of the attention Robert has paid other people rather than her. Coupled with her infatuation with Robert, she feels like she's starved for the special kind of attention he used to give her. The larger interesting aspect of this scene is that Edna doesn't know why she's upset--she herself is in denial about the depth of her true feelings.

2. Why do you think Mrs. Pontellier pursues a friendship with Mademoiselle Reisz?

Time:

5-7 minutes

Discussion:

Students could have a wide variety of different ideas in answers to this question, because it's somewhat unclear why Edna pursues a friendship with Mademoiselle Reisz -- in Chapter XX, Edna herself admits she is not sure if she actually likes the woman. Perhaps Edna feels like Mademoiselle Reisz provides the only substantive connection to Robert she actually has, since he writes letters to Mademoiselle. Edna often pores over the letter Robert writes to Mademoiselle Reisz, reading all the little details of his life and feeding her infatuation.

A second possibility is that Edna feels she can be more herself with Mademoiselle Reisz, often finding herself crying at the state of her life while Mademoiselle plays the piano. There are numerous examples of Edna telling her true feelings to Mademoiselle Reisz, when she feels that she has to hide them around everyone else. Third, Mademoiselle may embody a sense of freedom and independence that Edna just wants to be around as she is discovering her own independent desires and views about the world. Regardless of which of these options (or others!) students choose to discuss, encourage them to find and evaluate supporting textual evidence.

3. What do you think of the advice that Doctor Mandelet gives Mr. Pontellier about his wife? Would you tell Mr. Pontellier something different?

Time:

8-10 minutes

Discussion:

The Doctor suggests Mr. Pontellier not bother his wife for a while and try not to let her odd behavior and moods bother him. He argues that women are mysterious and complex, and men can't possibly decipher their enigmatic ways. He suggests that Mr. Pontellier bring Edna to New York if she'll go, and also cautions him that it may take several months for Edna to regain her usual temperament and behavior, but not to worry.

Since this question couples personal opinion with textual analysis, students may have all different kinds of reactions to the Doctor's advice, especially given his inner thoughts at the end of the chapter. In their answers, students should examine what they know about the Doctor. In addition, they should use textual evidence to support whether they think his advice is helpful or not, and then explain why they think other kinds of advice might be better (e.g. telling him to change his behavior or be more strict with his wife, etc.)

4. In Chapter XXII, after the Doctor's conversation with Mr. Pontellier, Chopin writes: "The Doctor would have liked during the course of the conversation to ask, 'Is there any man in the case?' but he knew his Creole too well to make such a blunder as that." What do you think this line means? How does it reflect the New Orleans high society social norms and conventions examined in the novel?

Time:

5-7 minutes

Discussion:

Just to review: when Mr. Pontellier stops by to meet with Doctor Mandelet, the Doctor tells Mr. Pontellier to simply give his wife some space and let her odd moods and behaviors pass. However, after Mr. Pontellier leaves, the Doctor considers what man might be causing Edna to act so unusually, but "knew his Creole too well to make such a blunder" as bringing this thought up to Léonce.

The clear implication of the question in Mandelet's mind and his hesitancy to actually speak that question aloud is that the suggestion there is a man in Mrs. Pontellier's life would set-off a fire-storm of controversy. In the New Orleans Creole culture of Chopin's time, women were supposed to be well-rounded, accomplished wives and mothers. Since the home was so traditionally important, women were meant to be happy to put aside their own desires to serve the needs of their husbands and children, and graciously manage the personal and social matters of the household with skill and ease. Madame Ratignolle is a great example of an ideal New Orleans Creole woman, wife, and mother.

The Doctor realizes that saying that Mrs. Pontellier was so flagrantly betraying the traditional duties of her role as woman, wife, and mother, would create conflict in her marriage with Mr. Pontellier. Furthermore, even the mention of such a notion, could undermine or tarnish the family's position in high society. Presumably, the Doctor hopes that Mrs. Pontellier will stop her presumed dalliance and return to being her old self, which included being a passable, if not amazing, wife and mother.

5. What do you the significance is of Edna's final thoughts related to her family in Chapter XXVI? How might these thoughts be related to her feelings for and exciting news about Robert? How might the thoughts be connected to her plans for her future as a self-sufficient artist?

Time:

8-10 minutes

Discussion:

When Edna leaves Mademoiselle Reisz's home, she decides to send candy to her children and a friendly letter to Mr. Pontellier. This happy and thoughtful consideration for her husband and children, while not unusual, is atypically positive for Edna when it comes to matters with her family.

Interestingly, just before Edna has these happy and positive thoughts about her family, she and Mademoiselle Reisz spoke about her feelings for Robert. In a recent letter he wrote to Mademoiselle, Robert said that he was returning to New Orleans shortly. Edna is overwhelmed with excitement to learn this news. Mademoiselle Reisz asks Edna seriously if she loves Robert too and, for the first time, Edna admits her true feelings. When Mademoiselle asks Edna to explain her feelings, she cannot -- she just knows she is in love with Robert. Since Edna does not yet seem to think of her feelings for Robert as mutually exclusive from her marriage and family life, her joy over this news might make her more excited than usual to be a more attentive wife and mother, as well.

A second potential reason that she could be happier about her husband and family than usual is that she has made a decision -- in her mind, if not yet in reality -- to move into her own house and claim some independence in her life. This sense of freedom and renewal could make her feel less constrained by other aspects of normal life.

Day 2 - Short Answer Evaluation

1. Where is Robert going when he leaves Grand Isle?

   _____

2. After Robert leaves Grand Isle, what do the other guests think of Edna's continued attachment to him?

   _____

3. What is the first traditional social obligation that Mrs. Pontellier decides not to attend to because she doesn't want to, causing her husband to become alarmed?

   _____

4. After Edna and Léonce's argument about Edna's shirking of her social duties, how does Edna react?

   _____

5. What activity does Edna want to spend the vast majority of her time doing?

   _____

6. What they first see Edna back in New Orleans, what do Victor and Madame Lebrun notice is different about her?

   _____

7. What does Edna usually do when she goes over to Mademoiselle Reisz's home?

   _____

8. What does Doctor Mandelet secretly think has really caused the changes in Edna Pontellier's mood and behavior?

   _____

9. Why doesn't Léonce Pontellier want to take the Colonel's advice to be more strict with his wife?

   _____

10. Around what activity do Mrs. Pontellier and Alcée Arobin begin their acquaintance and start to build their more intimate relationship?

    _____

Answer Key

1. He is going to Vera Cruz, Mexico to pursue business interests.
2. Everyone seems to think that Edna's attachment to Robert is unremarkable.
3. Edna abruptly decides not to hold her weekly reception to receive callers at the Pontellier home.
4. After the argument, Edna reflects that she would have been very troubled and shamed by such an argument in the past, but now she felt an "inward fire" and a sense of stubborn deliberation.
5. Edna wants to spend all her time painting and walking around, mostly in solitude.
6. Victor and Madame Lebrun remark how "ravishing" Edna looks, commenting that "the city atmosphere has improved her. Some way she doesn't seem like the same woman."
7. She and Mademoiselle Reisz spend time chatting, then she obsessively reads any new letters Robert has written to Mademoisele Reisz, while her hostess plays beautiful pieces on the piano; often, while she reads and listens to the music, she becomes very emotional both due to her strong feelings for Robert and because of Mademoiselle's beautiful piano playing.
8. He suspects that Edna may be romantically involved with another man.
9. Léonce is unsure about this recommendation, considering how the Colonel "coerced his own wife into her grave."
10. Edna and Alcée begin going the racetrack together to gamble.

Day 2 - Crossword Puzzle

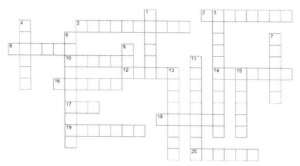

ACROSS

2. The name of the family doctor
5. Spacious, roomy, comfortable
8. Pamper, fawn over
10. Edna does not want to attend her _____'s wedding
12. A restorative medicinal drink
14. Edna's father is called the _____
16. Edna begins gambling on _____
17. Loud, alarming or unpleasant sound
18. Robert's business interested are located in _____
19. Where Léonce goes for his extended business trip
20. Something that is trivial or unimportant

DOWN

1. The nickname of Edna's new house
3. Argument, fight, quarrel
4. The surname of the renowned playboy
6. Depressed, dispirited, downcast
7. Plain or unattractive in appearance
9. As part of her pursuit of freedom, Edna wants to pursue _____
11. Means, method, tactic
13. Flirtatious manner or behavior
15. How does Edna ask Robert to communicate with her?

Crossword Puzzle Answer Key

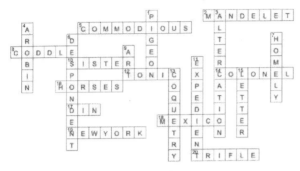

ACROSS

2. The name of the family doctor
5. Spacious, roomy, comfortable
8. Pamper, fawn over
10. Edna does not want to attend her _____'s wedding
12. A restorative medicinal drink
14. Edna's father is called the _____
16. Edna begins gambling on _____
17. Loud, alarming or unpleasant sound
18. Robert's business interested are located in _____
19. Where Léonce goes for his extended business trip
20. Something that is trivial or unimportant

DOWN

1. The nickname of Edna's new house
3. Argument, fight, quarrel
4. The surname of the renowned playboy
6. Depressed, dispirited, downcast
7. Plain or unattractive in appearance
9. As part of her pursuit of freedom, Edna wants to pursue _____
11. Means, method, tactic
13. Flirtatious manner or behavior
15. How does Edna ask Robert to communicate with her?

Day 2 - Vocabulary Quiz

Terms

1. _____ droll
2. _____ convulsively
3. _____ incipiently
4. _____ mulatto
5. _____ quizzical
6. _____ scintillant
7. _____ impetuosity
8. _____ delirium
9. _____ ennui
10. _____ consternation

Answers

A. insanity, madness, intoxicated or delusional disturbance
B. funny or comical in an unusual or peculiar manner
C. dismay, great concern, anxiety
D. full of something excitingly clever, skillful, or dazzling
E. someone who is of mixed black and white ethnic descent, usually one black and one white parent
F. with a sense of just awakening, dawning, or emerging
G. the quality of being impulsive, capricious, or rash
H. a sense of dissatisfaction, tedium, or listlessness, due to being understimulated
I. spasmodically; with sudden, violent movements
J. curious, puzzled (sometimes in an amused way)

Answer Key

1. B droll: funny or comical in an unusual or peculiar manner
2. I convulsively: spasmodically; with sudden, violent movements
3. F incipiently: with a sense of just awakening, dawning, or emerging
4. E mulatto: someone who is of mixed black and white ethnic descent, usually one black and one white parent
5. J quizzical: curious, puzzled (sometimes in an amused way)
6. D scintillant: full of something excitingly clever, skillful, or dazzling
7. G impetuosity: the quality of being impulsive, capricious, or rash
8. A delirium: insanity, madness, intoxicated or delusional disturbance
9. H ennui: a sense of dissatisfaction, tedium, or listlessness, due to being understimulated
10. C consternation: dismay, great concern, anxiety

Day 2 - Classroom Activities

1. Kate Chopin's Life and Times

Kind of Activity:

Long-term Project

Objective:

Students will be able to conduct research on life during the turn of the 20th century in the area around New Orleans and examine how societal changes may have impacted Chopin's life and writings.

Common Core Standards:

CCSS.ELA-Literacy.CCRA.R.4, CCSS.ELA-Literacy.CCRA.R.5

Time:

20-25 minutes (recurring)

Structure:

For an overview of this unit-long project, see the description in Day #1.

For Day #2, review the purpose of the activity and how it will continue through the unit. Then, demonstrate how to find important details from researching the world events and societal developments in America (and particularly the region around New Orleans) happening during Chopin's lifetime that could have impacted her perspectives about particular important themes in her writing.

Again, have each group select (or assign each group) a theme for the remainder of this project. Themes might include: history of the New Orleans region and "high society" culture in the late 19th and early 20th centuries; cultural expectations of women, marriage, and motherhood in this era; effects of Southern Reconstruction in the region during this period; developments in women's rights during this time period; Chopin's literary & philosophical influences and contemporaries; cultural/ religious reactions to the women's rights movement, etc..

Provide biographical sources on Chopin for students to read independently, or have them begin conducting their own research, depending on the time and resources available. These resources could include any of the following, in addition to many others:

New Orleans regional history:

- http://www.history.com/topics/new-orleans
- http://www.neworleansonline.com/neworleans/history/
- http://www.louisianafolklife.org/LT/Articles_Essays/ creole_art_creole_state.html
- http://www.neworleansonline.com/neworleans/multicultural/ multiculturalhistory/french.html
- http://www.museumofthecity.org/project/african-american-culture-in-new-orleans/
- http://www.neworleansonline.com/neworleans/multicultural/ multiculturalhistory/creole.html

Kate Chopin's life and writing:

- http://www.katechopin.org/
- https://americanliterature.com/author/kate-chopin/bio-books-stories
- http://www.pbs.org/katechopin/
- http://archive.vcu.edu/english/engweb/webtexts/hour/katebio.html
- http://docsouth.unc.edu/southlit/chopinawake/bio.html
- http://classiclit.about.com/library/bl-bio/bl-kchopin.htm

The Awakening and Kate Chopin's short stories Analysis:

- http://www.gradesaver.com/the-awakening
- http://www.litcharts.com/lit/the-awakening
- https://jwpblog.files.wordpress.com/2012/01/chopin-study-guide.pdf
- https://muse.jhu.edu/article/31709
- http://www.inquiriesjournal.com/articles/657/kate-chopins-the-awakening-struggle-against-society-and-nature
- http://www.katechopin.org/the-awakening/

Developments in Women's Rights & Societal Role at the turn of the 20th century:

- http://www.gilderlehrman.org/history-by-era/womens-history/essays/ women-american-politics-twentieth-century
- http://history.house.gov/Exhibitions-and-Publications/WIC/Historical-Essays/No-Lady/Womens-Rights/
- http://study.com/academy/lesson/feminism-in-the-19th-century-womens-rights-roles-and-limits.html
- https://www.nwhm.org/online-exhibits/progressiveera/suffrage.html
- http://www.enotes.com/topics/feminism/critical-essays/women-early-mid-20th-century-1900-1960

- http://www.loyno.edu/~kchopin/new/women/motherhood.html
- http://www.writereaderteacher.com/2013/06/gender-roles-in-late-1800s-and-early.html
- http://www.gilderlehrman.org/history-by-era/jackson-lincoln/essays/women-and-early-industrial-revolution-united-states

As in Day #1, the group scribe should chart the sociological events related to their group's theme, with a particular eye toward the ways that Day #2's readings have expanded their understanding of their assigned theme. Next, each group will examine the day's readings to find textual examples of the assigned theme. The group will then analyze their selected pieces of textual evidence and add them to their overall analysis.

Students will then share out one finding from their group with the whole class.

Ideas for Differentiated Instruction:

- Provide texts at a variety of reading levels depending on student ability.
- Provide some groups with the option to read aloud the biographical section, or listen to/watch audio or video pieces about Chopin as a form of research.
- Assign students different roles—scribe, head researcher, lead note-taker, presenter, etc.—based on skills or areas for growth.
- Split students into groups by skill-set or areas of need, so that some groups can work more independently, and the teacher can support other groups more.

Assessment Ideas:

- Student groups each generate a series of charts about an aspect of life or culture in Chopin's time and how it related to her writings, with specific references to *The Awakening* and Chopin's short stories.
- Student groups present findings from group chart to the rest of the class, while other students take notes in interactive handout on groups' presentations.
- Students complete a peer assessment of other group's presentations.

2. Exploring Creole Cultural History in New Orleans & Louisiana

Kind of Activity:

Research

Objective:

Students will be able to better understand Creole history and culture and their influence on the novel.

Common Core Standards:

CCSS.ELA-Literacy.CCRA.R.4, CCSS.ELA-Literacy.CCRA.R.6, CCSS.ELA-Literacy.CCRA.W.7, CCSS.ELA-Literacy.CCRA.W.8, CCSS.ELA-Literacy.CCRA.SL.4

Time:

30-35 minutes

Structure:

Although many of the themes in Chopin's novel are timeless and universal, the Creole cultural influences and references may be unfamiliar for many students. This activity will use multi-media resources to help students understand the cultural background for the novel.

Distribute a worksheet (paper or tablet) with designated areas for students to record reflections, evidence, and conclusions based on their experiences at each media station. Next, explain the various stations to the students. Stations may vary substantially by class needs, as well as time and resources available, but could include:

- **Image Analysis**: Images can be a powerful way for students to connect with and visualize a very different culture and history than their own. The first few pages of this e-book excerpt contain fascinating images that could be useful for contextualizing parts of the story and visualizing cultural influences. This website provides some images of Chopin and her life, while this site provides a number images related to the question "What is Creole?" A number of great historical images are also available on this website which explores the history of "The Louisiana Creole."
- **Literature Review**: Provide students with 2-3 excerpts to read or skim from books or articles that discuss the Creole culture, history, and place in society, as well as how these influences relate to *The Awakening*. This website provides links to many peer-reviewed articles about Creole culture and Kate Chopin's representation of that culture in her writing. Explore the sources available through this course. Have students read this article, published in 1883, which provides a brief but in-depth overview of Creole culture and explores how "Creole" is defined. These are only a few of the

many articles and resources available, and they vary significantly in complexity and reading level.

- **Film Excerpt Viewing**: There are a number of well-regarded documentaries available online giving histories of different parts of Creole culture and New Orleans area history, such as *The Creole controversy* and *Too White to be Black, Too Black to be White: The New Orleans Creole.* PBS provides an extensive list of documentaries about New Orleans and Creole culture.
- **Examining Excerpts from Kate Chopin's Private Papers**: Take selected sections from Kate Chopin's Private Papers, edited by Emily Toth and Per Seyersted, which includes a large number of Chopin's previously unpublished letters, journal entries, unpublished story segments, etc. This station is a great way for students to learn more about Chopin and practice examining challenging primary source material.
- **Independent Research**: Give students access to computers or additional documents to facilitate their own independent research on Creole culture and its place in New Orleans area history.

After students have completed all of the stations, bring the class back together to discuss what they discovered, as well as any theories they have about how these factors may have impacted Chopin's life and writings.

Ideas for Differentiated Instruction:

- Provide various levels of scaffolding in the worksheets and charts distributed to students—some can have additional questions or sentence starters to get students thinking about the right themes, others can have challenge or in-depth thinking questions.
- At the literature review station, give several different lengths of excerpts (or varying reading levels) to give students options for what to analyze.

Assessment Ideas:

- The worksheet/chart that students fill in during the stations activity can be turned in as an assessment.
- Students can complete a final quiz or writing assignment at the end of class, drawing connections between the different stations, to be turned in for grading.

3. Who Are You, Really?: Character Development in "The Awakening"

Kind of Activity:

Group Discussion

Objective:

Students will be able to examine the character traits and development of various players in the novel.

Common Core Standards:

CCSS.ELA-Literacy.CCRA.R.2, CCSS.ELA-Literacy.CCRA.R.4, CCSS.ELA-Literacy.CCRA.W.3, CCSS.ELA-Literacy.CCRA.SL.2

Time:

40-45 minutes

Structure:

Start out by having students identify each of *The Awakening*'s primary characters, using graphic organizers, note-taking templates, or chart paper to keep track of this information, and lead a brief discussion to identify 2-3 of each character's defining features.

After this short intro, split students into small groups and assign each group a main character to analyze. In this analysis, students should create the following categories: physical attributes, positive qualities of this character, negative qualities of this character (if applicable/known), relationships with others in the book, strengths and weaknesses of the character, and misconceptions others have about this character; other categories can be added, if desired. For each of these categories, students should find 2-3 stories, points, or pieces of text evidence picked out from which they'll develop a one-sentence summary (per category) about their overall sense of what this character is like in each of the categories above. Students can write their notes and analyses of different scenes in individual graphic organizers, or as a group in a chart or online note-taking template/document. If applicable for their group's character, students should make sure to consider in these summaries how the character seems to be changing over the course of the novel in personality, beliefs, world-view, feelings, etc.

After students complete their charts, have the groups present 2-3 particularly interesting points from their chart with the rest of the class. Finally, have students independently write short paragraphs reflecting on how their perception of their group's character changed or developed over the course of the novel.

NOTE: This activity should be completed before completing the "Inside Edition: Personal Views from *The Awakening*" activity from Day 3 of this lesson plan, which builds on groups' analyses and evaluations of their assigned characters', adding on a literary analysis and creative element.

Ideas for Differentiated Instruction:

- Split students into groups by skill-set or areas of need, so that some groups can work more independently, and the teacher can support other groups more (e.g. participating in the student discussion, helping to make connections, etc.).
- Assign students different roles—scribe, head researcher, lead note-taker, presenter, etc.—based on skills or areas for growth.
- For students who need additional support or ideas for how to fill out the chart and complete their character analyses, give students excerpts for research differentiated by reading level.

Assessment Ideas:

- Students individually complete the character chart and/or note-taking templates and submit for feedback.
- Students present findings from group chart/discussion to the rest of the class.
- Students submit individual final written analyses/reflections for assessment.

Day 3 - Reading Assignment, Questions, Vocabulary

Read *The Awakening*, Chapters XXVII-XXXIX (the end)

Common Core Objectives

- CCSS.ELA-Literacy.CCRA.R.2--Determine central ideas or themes of a text and analyze their development; summarize the key supporting details and ideas.

- CCSS.ELA-Literacy.CCRA.R.3--Analyze how and why individuals, events, or ideas develop and interact over the course of a text.

- CCSS.ELA-Literacy.CCRA.R.4--Interpret words and phrases as they are used in a text, including determining technical, connotative, and figurative meanings, and analyze how specific word choices shape meaning or tone.

- CCSS.ELA-Literacy.CCRA.W.3--Write narratives to develop real or imagined experiences or events using effective technique, well-chosen details and well-structured event sequences.

- CCSS.ELA-Literacy.CCRA.W.4--Produce clear and coherent writing in which the development, organization, and style are appropriate to task, purpose, and audience.

- CCSS.ELA-Literacy.CCRA.SL.1--Prepare for and participate effectively in a range of conversations and collaborations with diverse partners, building on others' ideas and expressing their own clearly and persuasively.

- CCSS.ELA-Literacy.CCRA.SL.3--Evaluate a speaker's point of view, reasoning, and use of evidence and rhetoric, identifying any fallacious reasoning or exaggerated or distorted evidence.

- CCSS.ELA-Literacy.CCRA.L.1--Demonstrate command of the conventions of standard English grammar and usage when writing or speaking.

Note that it is perfectly fine to expand any day's work into two days depending on the characteristics of the class, particularly if the class will engage in all of the suggested classroom exercises and activities and discuss all of the thought questions.

Content Summary for Teachers

"The Awakening," Chapter XXVII

Edna and Arobin are sitting together at her home and he is flirtatiously touching her hair and face. Edna is still filled with happiness, having just learned of Robert's return, so she speaks freely about many things that come into her mind. Edna and Arobin chat flirtatiously, and their talk turns to Mademoiselle Reisz. Edna mentions that Mademoiselle told her she would have to have "strong wings" if she wanted to fly above "the level plain of tradition and prejudice." Arobin responds by calling Mademoiselle crazy and then notes that Edna's thoughts seem to be somewhere else. They gaze at each other at length, and then Arobin kisses Edna. It is the first kiss of Edna's life that has made her feel anything, and it kindles desire within her.

"The Awakening," Chapter XXVIII

After Arobin's departure, various fluctuating emotions fill Edna's mind. Surrounded by all of the beautiful possessions Mr. Pontellier's provided for her, she feels guilt on account of her husband. However, the strongest feeling in her heart is a sense that she has betrayed her true, profound feelings for Robert. Overall, though, she thinks that this has been an enlightening experience and she feels no real sense of remorse or shame, although she is regretful that her infidelity was motivated by lust as opposed to love.

"The Awakening," Chapter XXIX

Without giving the matter another thought, Edna begins the move to the small house around the corner from the Pontelliers' grand home on Esplanade Street. She feels surrounded by her husband's possessions and needs her own space to build her own life. She starts to move all her own possessions to the "pigeon house."

Arobin walks into the house to find Edna atop a ladder taking pictures down from the wall, looking as vibrant and lively as ever. Arobin is not incredibly surprised by her unusual behavior, but he does try to get her to come down off the ladder. After his efforts are unsuccessful, he decides to help her.

Edna is concerned about being along with Arobin, so she tries to keep the maid nearby at all times. The couple talk about the fancy dinner party Edna is planning on throwing shortly to celebrate her move. After the celebration, Edna will complete her move into the "pigeon house." When Arobin tries to get time alone with Edna, she excuses herself to finish all the tasks she still has to complete and tells Arobin that she'll see him at the dinner. Arobin asks to see her sooner, but she refuses him.

"The Awakening," Chapter XXX

The grand dinner party turns out to be an intimate affair with a relatively small group of friends. The group sits around a lavishly decorated table, and Edna wears a shimmering gown and new diamond jewelry from her husband. Edna announces it's her twenty-ninth birthday and they drink to the Colonel's health while drinking cocktails of his creation.

Edna sits regally in her golden, shimmering gown as her guests chat jovially with each other. Although everyone seems to be having fun, Edna senses the familiar feeling of ennui and despair creeping up on her. She thinks about how she wants Robert, yet feels like she can't have him. Edna's guests continue to have fun together until Monsieur Ratignolle and Mademoiselle Reisz both decide it's time to leave. Mademoiselle tells Edna to be good on her way out the door.

When she re-enters the dining room, Mrs. Highcamp has begun weaving a garland of roses around Victor. As he poses, Edna is struck by the color contrasts and how handsome Victor is. Someone asks him to sing, and he begins to sing "Ah! si tu savais!" -- the song Edna associates with Robert -- and Edna gets worked up, accidentally breaking a wine carafe on the table. Victor apologizes to Edna and kisses her hand, and she asks him to stop performing for them. After this, the rest of the guests leave the lively party to head home in the still, silent street.

"The Awakening," Chapter XXXI

Arobin is the last remaining guest after the party disperses. After they lock up the Esplanade Street house, he offers to take Edna back to her "pigeon house," and they walk there arm-in-arm. Edna seems distant so they do not speak much, but when they arrive at the small house, Arobin comes in with her. Edna has already decorated a bit, so the house is cozy and welcoming. When she enters the pantry through the porch, she sees that Arobin has surprised her by having the pantry filled with flowers.

Edna tells Arobin that she feels exhausted and unwell, and he suggests that throwing the dinner at the end of such a hectic week might have worn her out. Edna agrees. Arobin offers to leave and let her rest, but as he does so, he smooths her hair and caresses her face with his hands. When Edna does not stop him, Arobin begins to kiss her shoulders and neck. Edna seems slightly worried by all this, and Arobin assures her that he'll leave after he says good night to her. Only after they sleep together does he finally bid her good-night.

"The Awakening," Chapter XXXII

Mr. Pontellier is extremely aggravated and disapproving when he learns of his wife's plans to move houses and neglect her responsibilities as a wife, mother, and member of the social elite. In order to dispel any unsavory rumors, Mr. Pontellier contracts a local architect to do a number of renovations on the house to make it clearly uninhabitable, and to demonstrate that they are financially sound. In addition, Mr. Pontellier has a local paper post a notice that the Pontelliers will be traveling for the summer while their house is under renovations.

Edna admires her husband's inventiveness, but otherwise does not pay much attention to what he is doing -- she simply enjoys the calm and peace of her new home. Feeling as if she's free of her obligations as part of the social elite, Edna experiences a new-found sense of independence, bordering on transcendence.

After a few days, Edna decides to go visit her children in Iberville. She spends a week there, playing with and enjoying the company of her children -- she finds that their youthful energy, simple love, and genuine curiosity about the world completely fulfills her while she is there. On her way back to New Orleans, Edna misses and longs for her children. However, once she returns to her "pigeon house," she feels happy again about the quiet solitude of her life there.

"The Awakening," Chapter XXXIII

Edna goes to visit Mademoiselle Reisz's flat to chat about Robert. As she waits for Mademoiselle, Edna remembers back to earlier in the day when Madame Ratignolle called on her to ask for help with her impending childbirth. She also cautioned Edna that she should be less rash in her decisions, and expresses concern about rumors she's heard of Arobin visiting Edna. Edna laughs off Madame Ratignolle's worries. Madame Ratignolle leaves, apologizing for even bringing up her concerns.

Coming back to the present, Edna casually occupies herself at Mademoiselle Reisz's apartment with the plants and piano as she waits. Suddenly, Robert knocks on the door and enters. Edna is surprised to learn that Robert had actually returned to New Orleans a couple of days prior, having left Mexico because he didn't get along with the people there.

Looking him over, Edna reflects that Robert hasn't changed much. When, for a brief moment, he looks deeply into her eyes, she remembers their time together at Grand Isle and recognizes the man she fell in love with the previous summer. She has envisioned her reunion with Robert so many times that she is a bit concerned at how awkward the actual meeting is. Rather than waiting for Mademoiselle Reisz's return, Robert and Edna go back to the "pigeon house" to have dinner. While at Edna's house, Robert sees a photograph of Alcée Arobin. Edna claims that she is using it to sketch from, and Robert asks if she knows Arobin. Edna redirects the conversation, and the pair end up casually and slightly flirtatiously talking about Grand Isle.

"The Awakening," Chapter XXXIV

Robert and Edna have a pleasant but mostly uninteresting dinner together. Robert begins to mention a woman he knows in Mexico, but then becomes awkward and downplays her significance. Arobin suddenly arrives and joins the couple, but Edna continues to insist on getting more information from Robert about the Mexican girl. Robert soon decides to leave. Arobin remains while she writes a letter, but then Edna tells him to leave because she wants to be alone. After his departure, she thinks back over every second of her time with Robert, becoming jealous of the Mexican girl and wondering if she and Robert were less intimate than she'd thought.

"The Awakening," Chapter XXXV

Edna awakens feeling only a sense of joy that she and Robert have reconnected, and wonders what he is up to. Letters from her husband and children arrive, which pleases her, as well as a message from Arobin, to which Edna does not reply. Edna is disappointed that Robert does not come to visit her for a few days, and one night, she accepts Arobin's invitation to go on a drive. They return to her home and sleep together before he bids her good-night. Edna feels very little when Arobin leaves her, nor does she feel happiness or excitement when she wakes in the morning.

"The Awakening," Chapter XXXVI

Edna frequents a small, secluded café out in the outskirts of New Orleans that is run by Catiche, an older mulatto woman. She finds the garden surroundings and wandering cat calming. One day, Robert unexpectedly appears at the café as well. Surprised to find her there, Robert awkwardly joins Edna at her table. Edna asks Robert why he's been avoiding her, and he responds with earnest but irritated questions about why she pushes him so and forces him to make excuses.

After they return to Edna's house, she kisses him and Robert finally admits that he's stayed away from Edna because of his love for her. Robert continues, saying that he knew he could not pursue Edna since she was married, and he imagined Leoncé setting her free to be with him. Edna corrects Robert's suggestion that she would become his possession in some way, explaining that she is now free and can give herself to whoever she wishes. Robert pales at this comment. At this moment, a maid comes to tell Edna that Madame Ratignolle is in labor. Edna says she must go, but asks Robert to wait there for her to return. As she readies herself to leave, Edna and Robert kiss passionately and she tells him that she loves him, that he had awakened her the previous summer, and that she can't wait for the to "be everything to each other." Robert pleads with her not to go, but she seductively tells him she'll return soon and leaves.

"The Awakening," Chapter XXXVII

Arriving at the Ratignolle house, Edna finds her friend suffering greatly and looking exhausted and ill. Madame Ratignolle screams about her husband and the doctor neglecting her when she is in so much pain. When the doctor does come, Madame Ratignolle refuses to let her friend leave, making Edna feel uncomfortable and reminding her of the disoriented terror she felt when she was in labor. She regrets having come, but doesn't feel like she can leave. Edna remains with Madame Ratignolle through her entire labor as if masochistically forcing herself to endure the pain with her friend. When Edna departs, Madame Ratignolle whispers to her, "Oh think of the children! Remember them!"

"The Awakening," Chapter XXXVIII

Leaving Madame Ratignolle's bedside, Edna feels dazed and uneasy, and Doctor Mandelet offers to accompany her home. While they walk, Edna confides in him about her conflicted feelings about motherhood and independence. She worries about the effect her actions might have on her children.

As she nears the "pigeon house," Edna gets excited remembering that Robert is waiting for her. She recalls Madame Ratignolle's warning to, "think of the children! Remember them!" (XXXVII), but decides to put it aside for the night. However, when she walks in, to her great sadness, she finds out that Robert has gone away, leaving only a short note that reads, "I love you. Good-by -- because I love you." Edna grows faint when she reads the note, and goes to lie down on the sofa. She lies there, awake and thinking, all night.

"The Awakening," Chapter XXXIX

The next and final chapter of *The Awakening* finds Victor back at Grand Isle, working on the cottages before guests arrive. Mariequita asks him questions, especially about Edna's party, and teases Victor about being in love with her. Unexpectedly, Edna arrives at the Lebrun estate, explaining only that she needed a little rest. Edna has realized that, even if she took a series of lovers and forgot about Robert, her responsibilities as a wife and mother would remain in her life, preventing her from fully experiencing freedom and independence.

Edna stops off at the beach house to put on her bathing suit. But when she stands alone in front of the ocean, she takes off the suit and stands on the beach, naked and alone, hearing the sea call to her seductively. Edna begins to swim out into the ocean without fear. She thinks of her friends and family and feels confident that they will never understand her need for independence. But then she realizes it is too late -- she has grown exhausted and is losing the will to keep swimming. Edna's last thoughts are from her youth: her father, the Colonel, and her sister, Margaret talking; an old dog barking; the cavalry officer she'd been infatuated with; and finally, the serene evening sounds and smells of her childhood.

Thought Questions (students consider while they read)

1. Why do you think Edna is initially unwilling to be left alone with Arobin after her first intimate encounter with him in Chapter XXXIX?

2. In what ways could the dinner party that Edna throws in Chapter XXX symbolize other aspects of her new-found independence? Does it foreshadow any of the events to come?

3. Why do you think Edna so enjoys visiting her children in Iberville so much? What has changed about their relationship and/or her situation that might impact her feelings about her children?

4. What do you make of Edna and Robert's surprise first meeting and subsequent dinner after months apart (Chapters XXXIII and XXXIV)? How is it different than Edna expected? Why do you think that might be?

5. Why do you think Edna returns to Grand Isle at the end of the novel?

Vocabulary (in order of appearance)

"'Well, that ought to be reason enough,' he acquiesced. 'You wouldn't give me another if I sat here all night imploring you.'" (Awakening, XXVII)

acquience:

accept or agree to something somewhat reluctantly

imploring:

begging, requesting earnestly or desperately

"It was only one phase of the multitudinous emotions which had assailed her." (Awakening, XXVIII)

multitudinous:

abundant, numerous

"If he had expected to find her languishing, reproachful, or indulging in sentimental tears, he must have been greatly surprised." (Awakening, XXIX)

languishing:

becoming feeble, weak, or lacking liveliness

"Ellen brought him one of her dust-caps, and went into contortions of mirth, which she found it impossible to control..." (Awakening, XXIX)

mirth:

high spirits, glee, amusement

"Mr. Merriman's laugh at this sally was such a genuine outburst and so contagious that it started the dinner with an agreeable swing that never slackened." (Awakening, XXX)

sally:

an outburst or rushing forth

In this context, the word likely means a joke or sly comment.

"Mrs. Highcamp hung with languid but unaffected interest upon the warm and impetuous volubility of her left-hand neighbor..." (Awakening, XXX)

languid:

relaxed, unhurried, showing little desire for exertion or effort

volubility:

the quality of talking excessively or incessantly

"...she felt the old ennui overtaking her; the hopelessness which so often assailed her, which came upon her like an

Day 3 - Reading Assignment, Questions, Vocabulary

obsession, like something extraneous, independent of volition." (Awakening, XXX)

volition:

will-power or faculty of free choice

"She was bien souffrante, and she was filled with vague dread, which only her husband's presence could allay." (Awakening, XXX)

allay:

diminish, calm, put to rest

"'Oh! to be able to paint in color rather than in words!' exclaimed Miss Mayblunt, losing herself in a rhapsodic dream as she looked at him." (Awakening, XXX)

rhapsodic:

rapturous, overflowing with emotion

"Back in the yard was room for servants, in which old Celestine had been ensconced." (Awakening, XXXI)

ensconce:

settle, install, establish

"There was to be an addition -- a small snuggery..." (Awakening, XXXII)

snuggery:

a comfy or cozy room or place

"...and she lingered occasionally to talk patois with Robert, whom she had known as a boy." (Awakening, XXXIV)

patois:

local dialect or regional vernacular

"He had detected the latent sensuality, which unfolded under his delicate sense of her nature's requirements like a torpid, torrid, sensitive blossom." (Awakening, XXXV)

torpid:

sluggish, lethargic, lacking mental or physical energy

torrid:

scorching, extremely hot and dry; very sultry or sensual

"'Why do you force me to idiotic subterfuges?' he exclaimed with sudden warmth." (Awakening, XXXVI)

subterfuge:

purposeful deception, intrigue, or trickery

"She leaned over and kissed him -- a soft, cool, delicate kiss, whose voluptuous sting penetrated his whole being..." (Awakening, XXXVI)

voluptuous:

luxuriously, sensually pleasurable

"The Doctor's coupé had returned for him and stood before the porte cochère." (Awakening, XXXVIII)

coupé:

a small, enclosed carriage

"...while the other women were all of them youthful houris, possessed of incomparable charms." (Awakening, XXXIX)

houri:

a beautiful, chaste young woman (traditionally, one of the virginal nymphs in Muslim paradise)

Additional Homework

1. Write a 1-2 page obituary for Edna Pontellier from the perspective of one of the other characters in *The Awakening*. In writing this piece, make sure to incorporate your understanding of events and characters from *The Awakening*, as well as your knowledge of the cultural and sociological setting for the novel.

Day 3 - Discussion of Thought Questions

1. Why do you think Edna is initially unwilling to be left alone with Arobin after her first intimate encounter with him in Chapter XXXIX?

Time:

5-7 minutes

Discussion:

Student answers to this question could vary widely and it could expand to a larger discussion of Edna's lack of understanding of her own feelings. After she sleeps with Arobin, Edna feels confused, guilty, and sad. However, the strongest feeling in her heart is a sense that she has betrayed her true, profound feelings for Robert. It is therefore understandable that Edna wants to avoid being alone with Arobin again, to avoid bringing up these same unpleasant feelings. She thinks that she should be more faithful to her love for Robert and, at least for the moment, believes that carrying on with Arobin would undermine or betray the true affection she feels for Robert.

2. In what ways could the dinner party that Edna throws in Chapter XXX symbolize other aspects of her new-found independence? Does it foreshadow any of the events to come?

Time:

8-10 minutes

Discussion:

Students could have a wide variety of different ideas in answers to this question as there are many possible parts of the dinner party scene that students could examine and evaluate in different ways. For instance, the fact that Edna's dinner party is so much smaller, calmer, and less lavish than she'd envisioned could be seen as a metaphor for the ways in which Edna's vision of freedom and independence is unrealistic for the actual world in which she lives. In addition, the guest list for the party is somewhat revealing -- while Edna does have some good friends there, some of those in attendance are people who the reader has previously learned have somewhat unsavory reputations in Edna's social circle. It is also notable that, despite the fact that her friends are having a lovely time, Edna is unable to escape the sense of disease and ennui that has haunted her intensely since the previous summer. Finally, although the dinner is meant to celebrate, in effect, the free and independent existence Edna thinks she wants, any reminder of Robert still upsets her. All of these examples, as well as many others students might pull out, suggest that Edna is not truly happy with her new life and foreshadows her ultimate submission to her new-found sense of freedom and the despair that accompanies it.

3. Why do you think Edna so enjoys visiting her children in Iberville so much? What has changed about their relationship and/or her situation that might impact her feelings about her children?

Time:

5-7 minutes

Discussion:

Since this question couples students' personal opinions about and understandings of Edna's mental state with textual analysis, students may have all different kinds of reactions to the Edna's visit to her children. Students should examine what they know about Edna's thoughts and emotional state throughout the novel, but especially in the chapters leading up to her visit to her children. Edna seems like she genuinely enjoys her children's company, but she struggles with the concept of giving herself fully and completely to her children. She loves doting on her children when she's with them, but she also relishes her life alone in which her time belongs to no one but her. Although, at this point, Edna seems to be able to maintain both sides of herself and both versions of her life simultaneously, she soon comes to realize that she cannot maintain both lives forever.

4. What do you make of Edna and Robert's surprise first meeting and subsequent dinner after months apart (Chapters XXXIII and XXXIV)? How is it different than Edna expected? Why do you think that might be?

Time:

8-10 minutes

Discussion:

These scenes clearly demonstrate that Edna and Robert's relationship is now much less intimate than Edna remembers it being. Edna has envisioned her reunion with Robert so many times that she is a bit concerned at how awkward the actual meeting is. Regardless of whether Edna and Robert's bond was every as strong as she'd imagined it to be, their interactions now are much more awkward, which makes one wonder why. Is Edna delusional? Did she imagine her bond with Robert? Was the bond true and Robert is just being withholding now? Does this have implications for other aspects of Edna's "awakening"? These are all questions students should consider as they discuss or think through this question. Thinking optimistically, one could imagine that perhaps Robert is just holding back and would soon make his feelings for Edna known, if given the right opportunity; however, although something like that does come to pass, Robert feels he must let Edna go anyway to allow her to have the freedom she seems to want. It seems possible that the awkwardness of Robert and Edna's meeting is meant to represent the entirety of Edna's "awakening" -- she hopes it will inspire and enlighten her, and allow her to live her life the way she wants, she finds instead that her dreams are untenable in the world she lives in.

5. Why do you think Edna returns to Grand Isle at the end of the novel?

Time:

5-7 minutes

Discussion:

Due to the open-ended nature of this question, students may have different opinions about why Edna makes the choices she does. Many students will likely argue that Mrs. Pontellier returned to the Grand Isle estate for the sole purpose of committing suicide; however, others may wonder at why she bothers conversing with Victor and Mariequita if she's only there to drown herself in the ocean. It is also possible that Edna had hoped that if she returned to Grand Isle, she would re-discover the magic she'd felt there the previous summer. When that magical sense of free will that awoke within her the previous summer cannot even be re-kindled in the place she found it originally, she realizes that she cannot continue to live in the world.

Day 3 - Short Answer Evaluation

1. What does Edna feel most guilty about after she and Arobin kiss?

   _____

2. Why can't Madame Ratagniolle attend Edna's dinner party?

   _____

3. How does Mr. Pontellier respond to his wife's plan to move to the smaller "pigeon house"?

   _____

4. What excuses does Mr. Pontellier set up to cover for his wife's sudden decision to move houses?

   _____

5. What does Madame Ratignolle make Edna promise?

   _____

6. Who surprises Edna when she is visiting Mademoiselle Reisz's flat?

   _____

7. Who gave Robert the embroidered tobacco pouch?

   _____

8. What does Robert say made him avoid being near Edna for so long?

   _____

9. What event unexpectedly calls Edna away from her revealing conversation with Robert?

_____

10. What happens to Edna at the end of the novel?

_____

Answer Key

1. Edna feels most guilty that she's betrayed her relationship with Robert.
2. She is heavily pregnant at this point in the novel.
3. Mr. Pontellier is angry and concerned about the reactions of the neighbors and others in their social circle.
4. Mr. Pontellier contracts a local architect to do renovations on the house to make it clearly uninhabitable, and demonstrate that they are financially sound.
5. Madame Ratignolle makes Edna promise to come to her when she goes into labor.
6. Robert Lebrun stops by to call on Mademoiselle Reisz, while Edna is already there waiting for Mademoiselle's return.
7. A Mexican woman in Vera Cruz, the significance of whom Robert downplays during his conversation with Edna.
8. Robert admits that his love for Edna kept him away from her for a long time.
9. Madame Ratignolle going into childbirth.
10. She commits suicide by swimming out deep into the ocean at Grand Isle.

Day 3 - Crossword Puzzle

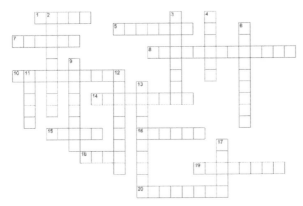

ACROSS

1. High spirits, glee, amusement
5. The mulatto woman who runs the small café on the outskirts of the city
7. The man Edna loves is _____
8. Abundant, numerous
10. Edna promises to attend to her friend _____ during childbirth
14. Begging, requesting earnestly or desperately
15. Edna's secret lover is _____
16. Local dialect or regional vernacular
18. At the end, Edna sees a _____ on the beach
19. Will-power or faculty of free choice
20. A comfy or cozy room or place

DOWN

2. Where the Pontellier children go to visit
3. Adèle tells Edna to "think of the _____!"
4. _____ sings a song that reminds Edna of her true love
6. Edna's last thoughts are of her _____
9. Settle, install, establish
11. Diminish, calm, put to rest
12. The name of the street the Pontelliers house is on
13. Luxuriously, sensually pleasurable
17. An outburst or rushing forth

Crossword Puzzle Answer Key

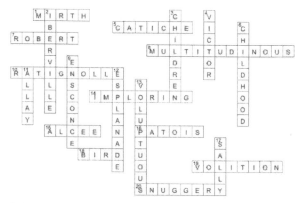

ACROSS

1. High spirits, glee, amusement
5. The mulatto woman who runs the small café on the outskirts of the city
7. The man Edna loves is _____
8. Abundant, numerous
10. Edna promises to attend to her friend _____ during childbirth
14. Begging, requesting earnestly or desperately
15. Edna's secret lover is _____
16. Local dialect or regional vernacular
18. At the end, Edna sees a _____ on the beach.
19. Will-power or faculty of free choice
20. A comfy or cozy room or place

DOWN

2. Where the Pontellier children go to visit
3. Adèle tells Edna to "think of the _____!"
4. _____ sings a song that reminds Edna of her true love
6. Edna's last thoughts are of her _____
9. Settle, install, establish
11. Diminish, calm, put to rest
12. The name of the street he Pontelliers house is on
13. Luxuriously, sensually pleasurable
17. An outburst or rushing forth

Day 3 - Vocabulary Quiz

Terms

1. _____ acquience
2. _____ languid
3. _____ volubility
4. _____ torpid
5. _____ torrid
6. _____ subterfuge
7. _____ houri
8. _____ coupé
9. _____ rhapsodic
10. _____ imploring

Answers

A. relaxed, unhurried, showing little desire for exertion or effort

B. rapturous, overflowing with emotion

C. begging, requesting earnestly or desperately

D. a beautiful, chaste young woman (traditionally, one of the virginal nymphs in Muslim paradise)

E. sluggish, lethargic, lacking mental or physical energy

F. the quality of talking excessively or incessantly

G. purposeful deception, intrigue, or trickery

H. accept or agree to something somewhat reluctantly

I. a small, enclosed carriage

J. scorching, extremely hot and dry; very sultry or sensual

Answer Key

1. H acquience: accept or agree to something somewhat reluctantly
2. A languid: relaxed, unhurried, showing little desire for exertion or effort
3. F volubility: the quality of talking excessively or incessantly
4. E torpid: sluggish, lethargic, lacking mental or physical energy
5. J torrid: scorching, extremely hot and dry; very sultry or sensual
6. G subterfuge: purposeful deception, intrigue, or trickery
7. D houri: a beautiful, chaste young woman (traditionally, one of the virginal nymphs in Muslim paradise)
8. I coupé: a small, enclosed carriage
9. B rhapsodic: rapturous, overflowing with emotion
10. C imploring: begging, requesting earnestly or desperately

Day 3 - Classroom Activities

1. Kate Chopin's Life and Times

Kind of Activity:

Long-term Project

Objective:

Students will be able to conduct research on life during the turn of the 20th century in the area around New Orleans and examine how societal changes may have impacted Chopin's life and writings.

Common Core Standards:

CCSS.ELA-Literacy.CCRA.R.4, CCSS.ELA-Literacy.CCRA.R.5

Time:

20-25 minutes (recurring)

Structure:

For an overview of this unit-long project, see the description in Day #1.

For Day #3, review the purpose of the activity and how it will continue through the unit. Then, have each group continue to research their assigned or selected theme. Again, themes might include: history of the New Orleans region; New Orleans "high society" culture during the turn of the 20th century; cultural expectations of women, marriage, and motherhood during this era; effects of Southern Reconstruction in the region during the late 19th and early 20th centuries; developments in women's rights during this time period; Chopin's Literary & Philosophical influences and contemporaries; Cultural/Religious Reactions to the women's rights movement, etc.

Provide biographical sources on Chopin for students to read independently, or have them begin conducting their own research, depending on the time and resources available. These resources could include any of the following, in addition to many others:

New Orleans regional history:

- http://www.history.com/topics/new-orleans
- http://www.neworleansonline.com/neworleans/history/
- http://www.louisianafolklife.org/LT/Articles_Essays/
  creole_art_creole_state.html
- http://www.neworleansonline.com/neworleans/multicultural/
  multiculturalhistory/french.html
- http://www.museumofthecity.org/project/african-american-culture-in-new-orleans/
- http://www.neworleansonline.com/neworleans/multicultural/
  multiculturalhistory/creole.html

Kate Chopin's life and writing:

- http://www.katechopin.org/
- https://americanliterature.com/author/kate-chopin/bio-books-stories
- http://www.pbs.org/katechopin/
- http://archive.vcu.edu/english/engweb/webtexts/hour/katebio.html
- http://docsouth.unc.edu/southlit/chopinawake/bio.html
- http://classiclit.about.com/library/bl-bio/bl-kchopin.htm

The Awakening and Kate Chopin's short stories Analysis:

- http://www.gradesaver.com/the-awakening
- http://www.litcharts.com/lit/the-awakening
- https://jwpblog.files.wordpress.com/2012/01/chopin-study-guide.pdf
- https://muse.jhu.edu/article/31709
- http://www.inquiriesjournal.com/articles/657/kate-chopins-the-awakening-struggle-against-society-and-nature
- http://www.katechopin.org/the-awakening/

Developments in Women's Rights & Societal Role at the turn of the 20th century:

- http://www.gilderlehrman.org/history-by-era/womens-history/essays/
  women-american-politics-twentieth-century
- http://history.house.gov/Exhibitions-and-Publications/WIC/Historical-Essays/No-Lady/Womens-Rights/
- http://study.com/academy/lesson/feminism-in-the-19th-century-womens-rights-roles-and-limits.html
- https://www.nwhm.org/online-exhibits/progressiveera/suffrage.html
- http://www.enotes.com/topics/feminism/critical-essays/women-early-mid-20th-century-1900-1960
- http://www.loyno.edu/~kchopin/new/women/motherhood.html
- http://www.writereaderteacher.com/2013/06/gender-roles-in-late-1800s-and-early.html
- http://www.gilderlehrman.org/history-by-era/jackson-lincoln/essays/
  women-and-early-industrial-revolution-united-states

As in Days #1 & 2, the group scribe should chart the sociological events related to their group's theme, with a particular eye toward the ways that Day #2's readings have expanded their understanding of their assigned theme. Next, each group will examine the day's readings to find textual examples of the assigned theme. The group will then analyze their selected pieces of textual evidence and add them to their overall analysis.

Students will then share out one finding from their group with the whole class.

Ideas for Differentiated Instruction:

- Provide texts at a variety of reading levels depending on student ability.
- Provide some groups with the option to read aloud the biographical section, or listen to/watch audio or video pieces about Chopin as a form of research.
- Assign students different roles—scribe, head researcher, lead note-taker, presenter, etc.—based on skills or areas for growth.
- Split students into groups by skill-set or areas of need, so that some groups can work more independently, and the teacher can support other groups more.

Assessment Ideas:

- Student groups each generate a series of charts about an aspect of life or culture in Chopin's time and how it related to her writings, with specific references to *The Awakening* and Chopin's short stories.
- Student groups present findings from group chart to the rest of the class, while other students take notes in interactive handout on groups' presentations.
- Students complete a peer assessment of other group's presentations.

2. Turning Points in "The Awakening"

Kind of Activity:

Group Discussion

Objective:

Students will be able to identify and analyze important turning points that take place in the novel.

Common Core Standards:

CCSS.ELA-Literacy.CCRA.R.1, CCSS.ELA-Literacy.CCRA.R.2, CCSS.ELA-Literacy.CCRA.W.2

Time:

35-40 minutes

Structure:

In this activity, students will work in small groups to chart out all of the important events in *The Awakening*, and analyze specific turning points in the characters' stories or lives. Split students into small groups and distribute guided handouts that ask questions about important moments or turning points like:

- What happened in this moment?
- Why was it important?
- Who was impacted by this event?
- What impact did this event/moment have on this person's life/relationships/beliefs?

Have each group of students continue building their own timeline for events in the story until they have at least 8-12 different important scenes/events/turning points in the novel. For each point on the timeline, students should include a brief explanation of why it's important and how it impacts the story. Students could create this timeline using various online resources (such as http://www.dipity.com/ or a shared online document), on chart paper, or in individual graphic organizers.

After students have finished adding to their timelines, have each student select 2-3 "turning point" moments on their group's (or other group's) timeline that they think are particularly important for the story/characters: 2-3 points at which a character did or said one thing that ultimately impacted their lives dramatically. Have students take notes individually on why they think these points are particularly important. Then have students discuss in pairs or small groups why students' think certain moments are particularly pivotal for the story. Finally, in class or as a homework assignment, have students write a 1-2 paragraph analysis of one of the turning points of the novel, why it's important, and how it might have turned out differently if the character in question had thought/acted/spoken differently.

Ideas for Differentiated Instruction:

- Group students in small groups by different skill sets and areas for growth.
- Give bonus/challenge questions to students who are particularly skilled at literary analysis

- Provide students with different ways to engage with the material if necessary (listening to it, read aloud, visual representations of different important points in the story, etc.)

Assessment Ideas:

- Students fill out individual guided handouts about the important points their groups are including on their timelines, which can be submitted and graded.
- Students individual writing assignments evaluating "turning points" should be submitted for evaluation.
- Groups' timelines can be evaluated and graded.
- Assess students' participation in their group's work and the extent to which they participate in the discussion.

3. Inside Edition: Personal Views from "The Awakenining"

Kind of Activity:

Collaborative Writing

Objective:

Students will be able to evaluate events in the novel from the perspectives of various characters.

Common Core Standards:

CCSS.ELA-Literacy.CCRA.R.3, CCSS.ELA-Literacy.CCRA.W.3

Time:

60-70 minutes total (best done in 2 separate 30-35 minute parts on different days)

Structure:

This activity is somewhat long and complex, and could easily be split into 2 separate days--the first evaluating the voices of different characters in the novel, and the second creating journal or diary entries from the perspectives of these characters. In addition, it is important to complete this activity after doing the "Who Are You,

Really?: Character Development in 'The Awakening'" classroom activity from Day 2 of this lesson plan or an in-depth class-wide discussion and analysis of the novel's major characters. This activity assumes students already have a fairly solid understanding of the background, beliefs, feelings, and ways of thinking about the world of all major characters in the novel, and it'll be harder for students to make these entries authentic if they're not sure about how the characters think. If students have not completed the "Who Are You, Really?: Character Analysis" activity from Day 2, split them into 5-6 small groups and assign an *Awakening* main character to each group for analysis.

In addition, this activity extends the "Turning Points in *The Awakening*" classroom activity, also from Day 3 of this lesson plan. If that activity is not completed before this one, provide students with specific scenes/events/turning points in the novel that they will write about from their character's perspective in Part II of this activity.

Part I: Creating Character "Voice" Arc

Building on the "Who Are You, Really?" activity from Day 2, students should be split into the same groups as in that activity so that they will continue analyzing the same character. Students will be examining the perspective and voice of their character and writing notes in a graphic organizer, chart paper, or online shared document (e.g. Google Docs) about the important elements of their character's "voice."

If the concept of "voice" -- specifically an understanding of character "voice" as opposed to the author's "voice" -- is new for the students, provide a definition and have a brief discussion about what it means and how it appears in the novel. "Voice" can be understood as the language and words that each character uniquely uses to convey their personality and opinions in the story. In *The Awakening*, the voices of many main characters are made more complex and interesting by the addition of many passages, interspersed with informative and telling dialogue sections, in which the narrator talks about how each character views the world and his or her life at different points in the story using distinct kinds of language for each character.

Have students take a few minutes to review the character traits and elements they analyzed and discussed in the "Who Are You, Really?" activity from Day 2. Then have them examine their character's actions, words, and descriptions at various points throughout the novel. They could start with any points they think are important in the story, such as those they may have found and discussed in the "Turning Points in *The Awakening*" classroom activity earlier in Day 3. As part of their analysis, students should examine at least two different elements: how the character herself or himself speaks and how the narrator talks about this character's thoughts, ideas, and feelings. Students should select approximately 8-12 scenes/ events/turning points in the novel to discuss and analyze. Then, have students create a timeline or map of how the characters develop over the course of the novel, adding in any transitional moments they think are important, to create an overall character "voice" arc.

This section of this activity can be presented by the groups to the rest of the class at this point or later with Part II of the activity.

<u>Part II: Writing Character's Journal/Diary Entries</u>

Students should use the 8-12 (or more, if desired) scenes/events/turning points selected in Part I and, using their analysis of these points in the novel, write journal/ diary entries from their group's character's perspective. Students could write these journal/diary entries in hard-copy form (e.g. physically writing journal entries as their character would have), write them collaboratively or individually in a shared online document (e.g. Google Docs), or create a blog written from their character's perspective.

Have students complete at least 8-12 total journal/diary entries, either collaboratively or split up between individual students in each group, in either hard copy or digital form. Students' entries should be written from the perspective and in the voice of their group's character and reflect any ways in which those aspects of their group's character changes over the course of the novel. Of course, students could complete this activity over multiple days or have whatever journal/diary entries they don't finish assigned for homework. In addition, this is a great activity to include a peer review/feedback element to help students refine their writing.

After students have completed the character-voice journal/diary entries, groups should prepare a presentation or performance of some kind of these entries for the other students. This presentation for Part II could be free-standing, or this assignment could be a culmination presentation paired with the groups' character personality/ world-view analysis in the "Who Are You, Really?" activity from Day 2 and the character "voice" examination in Part I of this activity.

Ideas for Differentiated Instruction:

- Provide students with various levels of scaffolding (hints, sentence starters, etc.) in their guided handouts in order to facilitate deeper understanding of their groups' assigned characters for students of different levels of literary analysis.
- Group students based on their particular skills or areas for growth
- Assign roles to different students in the groups (scribe, head researcher, presenter, editor, etc.) in order to build on some students' unique skills and provide challenges to others.
- Provide groups with a variety of options -- written, digital slideshow presentation, multimedia, artistic, performance, etc. -- for how they can choose to present their character to the rest of the class.
- Members of each student group could contribute different types of media to the group's character presentation(s) to reflect their different interest areas/skills.

Assessment Ideas:

- Any worksheets/charts/shared notes that students take during this activity can be turned in as an assessment.
- Students' journal/diary entries can be submitted for peer review & editing and/or teacher assessment.
- Students' final presentations can be graded as separate assignments for Part I & II of this activity, or combined with assessments from the other activities on which this activity builds.
- Students can complete a final quiz or writing assignment at the end of this activity to provide an opportunity for personal reflection on a mostly group analysis assignment.

Day 4 - Reading Assignment, Questions, Vocabulary

Read "A Respectable Woman," "Athénaïse," and "The Story of an Hour"

Common Core Objectives

- CCSS.ELA-Literacy.CCRA.R.1--Read closely to determine what the text says explicitly and to make logical inferences from it; cite specific textual evidence when writing or speaking to support conclusions drawn from the text.

- CCSS.ELA-Literacy.CCRA.R.2--Determine central ideas or themes of a text and analyze their development; summarize the key supporting details and ideas.

- CCSS.ELA-Literacy.CCRA.R.4--Interpret words and phrases as they are used in a text, including determining technical, connotative, and figurative meanings, and analyze how specific word choices shape meaning or tone.

- CCSS.ELA-Literacy.CCRA.R.10--Read and comprehend complex literary and informational texts independently and proficiently.

- CCSS.ELA-Literacy.CCRA.W.7--Conduct short as well as more sustained research projects based on focused questions, demonstrating understanding of the subject under investigation.

- CCSS.ELA-Literacy.CCRA.W.8--Gather relevant information from multiple print and digital sources, assess the credibility and accuracy of each source, and integrate the information while avoiding plagiarism.

- CCSS.ELA-Literacy.CCRA.SL.1--Prepare for and participate effectively in a range of conversations and collaborations with diverse partners, building on others' ideas and expressing their own clearly and persuasively.

- CCSS.ELA-Literacy.CCRA.SL.4--Present information, findings, and supporting evidence such that listeners can follow the line of reasoning and the organization, development, and style are appropriate to task, purpose, and audience.

Note that it is perfectly fine to expand any day's work into two days depending on the characteristics of the class, particularly if the class will engage in all of the suggested classroom exercises and activities and discuss all of the thought questions.

Content Summary for Teachers

"A Respectable Woman"

Mrs. Baroda learns that Gouvernail -- a friend of her husband, Gaston -- is visiting the couple's plantation for a week or two. Mrs. Baroda is displeased about this news, as she had hoped to have time with her husband to recuperate after a busy winter. Although Mrs. Baroda hasn't met Gouvernail, she knows that he and her husband were college friends and that he now works as a journalist. Mrs. Baroda imagines Gouvernail as a skinny, cynical fellow -- an image that does not appeal to her -- but upon meeting him, actually enjoys his company.

Although Mrs. Baroda likes Gouvernail well enough, she cannot figure out why Gaston had described him as brilliant. Other than being generally pleasant, Gouvernail does not try to endear himself to Mrs. Baroda in any other way. He spends most of his time sitting on the porch and talking with Gaston about the plantation.

Mrs. Baroda finds Gouvernail's reticent nature curious, and initially leaves him and Gaston to spend time together on their own. However, she soon begins going on walks with Gouvernail to try to better comprehend his enigmatic personality.

Mrs. Baroda considers going to the city for a while to stay with her aunt. As she sits contemplating, Gouvernail joins her and opens up about his desire for some peace in his current life. It is Gouvernail's voice rather than his words that especially catch Mrs. Baroda's attention, and she considers drawing him closer to her. She is only able to resist this impulse because she is "a respectable woman." Mrs. Baroda eventually leaves Gouvernail to finish telling his thoughts to the night on his own.

Mrs. Baroda considers telling her husband about the draw she felt towards Gaston, but then realizes it would be more prudent to handle her feelings alone. The following day, Mrs. Baroda departs for New Orleans and remains there until after Gouvernail leaves. Gaston tells his wife that he'd like Gouvernail to come stay again the following summer, but she says no. Later, however, to her husband's delight, she changes her mind. Gaston tells his wife that Gouvernail never deserved her dislike of him. Mrs. Baroda responds by kissing him and saying that she has "overcome everything" and that she'll be kinder to Gouvernail in the future.

"Athénaïse"

The story begins with Cazeau, a man recently married to a young woman named Athénaïse, learning that his new wife has gone back to her parents' home. Cazeau goes to try to retrieve Athénaïse. On the way, he meets his brother-in-law, Monteclin, who clearly despises him and tells him to stay away. When he gets to his parents-in-law's house, however, they welcome him in. It turns out that Cazeau is not a bad husband to Athénaïse, nor does he mistreat her in any way; she simply doesn't like being married. Despite this, when Cazeau says it's time to leave, she agrees to go with him.

Athénaïse continues to be extremely displeased with her situation: married to a man for whom she feels no passionate love. With the help of her brother, she begins to plot her escape. In the meantime, Cazeau resolves not to fight for a woman who no longer feels strongly for him. Athénaïse escapes to New Orleans and lives in a guest-house of sorts there. Sylvie, the owner, looks after Athénaïse, and Gouvernail, a single man also staying as a guest at the house, befriends her. Athénaïse finds her friendship with Gouvernail comforting in a brotherly, platonic sort of way, while Gouvernail plans to seduce Athénaïse and have an affair with her.

However, everything changes suddenly when Athénaïse realizes that she is pregnant. The unexpected news completely alters Athénaïse's perspective on her marriage and her husband. Athénaïse feels as if "her whole being was stepped in a wave of ecstasy"; and when she thinks about Cazeau, she feels "her whole passionate nature aroused as if by a miracle." Athénaïse promptly returns to her husband. When Athénaïse and Cazeau kiss upon seeing each other again, Cazeau feels "her lips for the first time respond to the passion of his own."

"The Story of an Hour"

Due to a heart condition, Louise Mallard must be told about her husband's death in a careful manner. Josephine, Louise's sister, breaks the news to her. Louise is shocked and begins crying uncontrollably upon hearing about his death. She retreats to her room upstairs to be alone.

As Louise sits quietly and looks out an open window, she observes the outside world with all her senses -- she sees trees beginning to blossom, smells a storm approaching, and hears a salesman selling his wares on the street. Then she notices someone singing outside, the sparrows calling to each other as they flit about the eaves of houses, and the big fluffy clouds in the sky. Although she feels grief and shock, she also begins to feel something like relief, and a sense of freedom.

Louise reflects that she'll weep again when she actually sees her husband's body -- he was a good, loving, kind husband to her. But as she thinks about the years she has ahead of her, which are now hers alone to spend as she wishes, she spreads her arms to welcome that new life. Louise relishes the thought of being free and able to "live for herself," with no other person's will or desires to oppress her any longer. She considers how men and women oppress each other, even if they do so out of love.

Josephine comes to check on Louise, warning her that she'll make herself sick if she doesn't come out of her room. Louise tells Josephine to go away. She then imagines all the things she'll do with the days and years of independence she has ahead of her, and hopes she'll have a long life. After some time, she gave in to her sister's entreaties to open the door, and she and Josephine begin to go down stairs, where her husband's friend is waiting.

Suddenly, the front door opens, and Louise's husband walks in. He is slightly disheveled from his trip, but hasn't been killed in a train accident and didn't even know one took place. Louise collapses from the schok. When doctors arrive, they say Louise died of a heart attack brought on by joy.

Thought Questions (students consider while they read)

1. In "A Respectable Woman," what do you think it is about Gouvernail that initially makes Mrs. Baroda unsure about having him stay?

2. Why do you think Mrs. Baroda changes her mind about having Gouvernail return the following summer?

3. What makes "Athénaïse" unique among Chopin's stories? Why are these differences significant?

4. What do you think of Gouvernail as a character? How is he different than most of the men Kate Chopin writes?

5. In "The Story of an Hour," why do you think Louise Mallard's perspective on her husband's death shifts so drastically as she sits and thinks by herself?

Vocabulary (in order of appearance)

"She was looking forward to a period of unbroken rest, now, and undisturbed te ˆ te-a-te ˆ te with her husband..." (A Respectable Woman)

te ˆ te-a-te ˆ te:

a private talk between two people; a heart-to-heart

"Once settled at the plantation he seemed to like to sit upon the wide portico in the shade of one of the big Corinthian pillars..." (A Respectable Woman)

portico:

a structure with a roof supported by columns spaced regularly, often attached to a building (e.g. a wraparound porch)

"He did not care to fish, and displayed no eagerness to go out and kill grosbecs when Gaston proposed doing so." (A Respectable Woman)

grosbec:

A French term meaning any bird with a large beak, presumably ones that are typically hunted.

"...she imposed her society upon him, accompanying him in his idle strolls to the mill and walks along the batture." (A Respectable Woman)

batture:

the often rocky, damp area along the banks or in the middle of a river where the land rises out of the water at times and is submerged at other times

"He kissed her and turned to fasten his cravat before the mirror." (A Respectable Woman)

cravat:

a wide, short strip of fabric worn by men around the neck and tucked into the neck of a shirt; similar to a neck-tie

"He made some commonplace observation upon the baneful effect of the night air at that season." (A Respectable Woman)

baneful:

destructive or harmful

"She made no reply to this apostrophe to the night, which indeed, was not addressed to her." (A Respectable Woman)

apostrophe:

a literary term meaning an address given by a speaker who has detached himself to reality and is speaking to an imaginary character or idea of some kind

"Gouvernail was in no sense a diffident man, for he was not a self-conscious one." (A Respectable Woman)

diffident:

modest, shy, unassuming

"Athénaïse went away in the morning to make a visit to her parents, ten miles back on rigolet de Bon Dieu." (Athénaïse)

rigolet:

a small rivulet or creek

"...the task of bringing his wife back to a sense of her duty seemed to him for the moment paramount." (Athénaïse)

paramount:

vital, supremely important

"'Cochon!' he muttered under his breath as Cazeau mounted the stairs,—'sacré cochon!'" (Athénaïse)

cochon:

the French word for "pig"

"But if there was no way of untying this Gordian knot of marriage, there was surely a way of cutting it." (Athénaïse)

Gordian knot:

an extremely challenging or difficult problem

"'I have not had the time, the leisure, to devote to her training; and what good we might have accomplished, that maudit Montéclin...'" (Athénaïse)

maudit:

a poet or bohemian living a life against or outside of society, often associated with someone who is an addict, criminal, or mentally unsound

"This was said with unusual asperity. It was the little breach that Athénaïse had been watching for, and she charged rapidly..." (Athénaïse)

asperity:

sharpness, harshness, or abrasiveness

"It was really all one to her that her mistress returned them to her keeping, and refused to take further account of the menage" (Athénaïse)

menage:

household or domestic establishment

"It was not a plan which met with instant favor, which she was at once ready to accept, for it involved secrecy and dissimulation, hateful alternatives, both of them." (Athénaïse)

dissimulation:

pretense or deceit in showing one's thoughts, character, or feelings

"...a dignity that in the presence of white people assumed a character of respectfulness, but never of obsequiousness." (Athénaïse)

obsequiousness:

the quality of showing deference or subservient complacence

"Athénaïse was really not so exhausted as she had every reason to be after that interminable and circuitous way..." (Athénaïse)

interminable:

never-ending, endless

"He lounged about, gathered a rose for his buttonhole, and had his regular Sunday-morning confab with Pousette..." (Athénaïse)

confab:

an informal, but usually private chat or discussion

"...he was confronted by Athénaïse, exhibiting some confusion and trepidation at being forced to request a favor of him at so early a stage of their acquaintance." (Athénaïse)

trepidation:

apprehension, dread, fear

"She wondered a little at a man of his supposed erudition stumbling over the spelling of 'Montéclin' and 'Miché.'" (Athénaïse)

erudition:

Day 4 - Reading Assignment, Questions, Vocabulary

possessing or demonstrating great knowledge, scholarship, or intellect

"What was it? She did not know; it was too subtle and elusive to name." (The Story of an Hour)

elusive:

hard to catch, find, or remember

"Now her bosom rose and fell tumultuously." (The Story of an Hour)

tumultuously:

with great disturbance or uproar

Additional Homework

1. Examine and analyze 3-4 of the previously unexamined documents in the *Kate Chopin's Private Papers.* In a 2-3 page essay, discuss how these documents reveal more about Kate Chopin and the inspiration for her writing.

Day 4 - Discussion of Thought Questions

1. In "A Respectable Woman," what do you think it is about Gouvernail that initially makes Mrs. Baroda unsure about having him stay?

Time:

5-7 minutes

Discussion:

Student answers to this question may vary as Mrs. Baroda gives several vague reasons for not really particularly liking Gouvernail. However, Mrs. Baroda's change of heart about Gouvernail late in the story suggests that perhaps she is wary around her husband's friend because she can't figure him out.

Mrs. Baroda feels a sense of intrigue and mystery when she is around Gouvernail that is both alluring and uncomfortable to her. It is notable that Mrs. Baroda has been entertaining all winter and seems to be someone who shares most of her thoughts and feelings with her husband. These small references in the story could indicate that Chopin intends the reader to see Mrs. Baroda as a typical and ideal New Orleans Creole high society woman -- happy to entertain, pleasant, fulfills her social obligations, doting wife (and presumably mother), etc. Gouvernail is not like that. He wants to have peace from his hectic life and is not open with his feelings or thoughts. His quiet, reserved nature seems to intrigue Mrs. Baroda, but it also makes her nervous, perhaps because she is afraid of becoming too interested and inviting gossip.

2. Why do you think Mrs. Baroda changes her mind about having Gouvernail return the following summer?

Time:

8-10 minutes

Discussion:

Again, students may have a wide variety of answers to this question, because it is left purposefully unclear and ambiguous. Indeed, readers and critics alike have long debated the meaning of the ending. Some students might think that Mrs. Baroda's final declaration is a suggestion that she has conquered her unruly attractions and will be now be fine having Gouvernail as a guest. She says she has overcome "everything," which could suggest she's overcome her resistance to the idea of him staying as well as getting past her hard-to-understand dislike of him. However, other students might have another, less socially acceptable interpretation. Although Chopin leaves the meaning of Mrs. Baroda's final line unclear, from what students know about Chopin's views of female sexuality and independence, they might infer that she has overcome her reservations about exploring her own desires and inner workings. Gouvernail seemed to slightly awaken something in Mrs. Baroda, and what she may be saying she has "overcome" is her desire to conform to societal expectations of her thoughts and behavior.

3. What makes "Athénaïse" unique among Chopin's stories? Why are these differences significant?

Time:

8-10 minutes

Discussion:

Many students might think of this story as an alternate (and most think, less compelling) version of *The Awakening* -- both stories have very similar sets of characters and women with similar motivations. However, in "Athénaïse," readers see both Athénaïse and Cazeau as protagonists in some ways and there is much more insight given into the mindsets, thoughts, feelings, and beliefs of male characters, including both Cazeau and Gouvernail. This is out of character for Chopin's writing. In addition, the conclusion of the story is unique among Chopin's stories, as the idea of motherhood seems to transform Athénaïse from a woman who wants to be single and free into a happy, complacent wife and mother-to-be. This view of marriage, childbirth, and motherhood is also different than the ideas Chopin puts forth in her other writings.

Critics tend to divide on the significance of "Athénaïse," so students will likely do the same. Some critics think the story is lacking and just a less interesting version of part of *The Awakening*. Those in this camp tend to think the story has a disappointing ending that gives in to commonplace expectations of women's role in the world. Others argue that this is one of Chopin's most fleshed-out and robust stories, a warm-up to *The Awakening* in which she examines a woman following her desires and instincts and how that woman's decisions impact those around her. In this reading of the story, Athénaïse's character and choices are just one part of the story; the other characters and their inner monologues play just as significant a role in how the story develops. The insights into the minds of multiple characters also makes "Athénaïse" unique among most of Chopin's stories other than *The Awakening*.

4. What do you think of Gouvernail as a character? How is he different than most of the men Kate Chopin writes?

Time:

5-7 minutes

Discussion:

Most of the men that Kate Chopin portrays in her stories are high society gentleman, successful in business and with satisfying personal and social lives, but without any clear indications of having significant inner thoughts, feelings, or ideas that aren't already outwardly obvious. Gouvernail is one of a few male characters in Chopin's stories who is different.

Gouvernail is an important character in "A Respectable Woman" and "Athénaïse," as well as making a cameo appearance in *The Awakening*. He is a thoughtful, sensitive, intelligent, introspective person who seeks to form friendships (and maybe more intimate relationships) with several women. In most cases, the only characters that Chopin portrays in her stories that have these same qualities are women, making Gouvernail an especially unique character. Chopin is clearly trying to explore the mindset and perspective of a man who possesses many of the enigmatic thoughts that many of her female characters have.

5. In "The Story of an Hour," why do you think Louise Mallard's perspective on her husband's death shifts so drastically as she sits and thinks by herself?

Time:

5-7 minutes

Discussion:

Students might argue that Louise is simply in shock and unsure how to feel about her husband's death. Other students might suggest that, upon experiencing with her own senses the vast world outside her house (and by association, outside her marriage), Louise realizes everything she's been missing this whole time and how much there is in the world for her to explore and experience now that she no longer has marital obligations. Louise also suggests that she never really loved her husband all that much, which leads one to believe that, like many other women in Chopin's stories, she views her marriage as more of a social obligation than a union with someone she feels passion for. Other students may think that the ending complicates the interpretation, since Louise dies of a heart attack brought on by joy upon seeing her husband alive.

Day 4 - Short Answer Evaluation

1. In what two stories does the character Gouvernail appear?

   _____

2. In "A Respectable Woman," where is Mr. Baroda's friend planning to come visit the Barodas?

   _____

3. What allows Mrs. Baroda to overcome her desire to draw her husband's friend close to her during their one serious conversation?

   _____

4. Who helps Athénaïse escape her unhappy marriage in "Athénaïse"?

   _____

5. Where does Athénaïse go to stay when she leaves her marital home?

   _____

6. What sort of relationship does Athénaïse develop with the man she meets at the boarding house?

   _____

7. What new information causes Athénaïse to joyfully return to her husband?

   _____

8. In "The Story of an Hour," how did Louise Mallard's husband supposedly die?

   _____

9. How does Louise feel when she learns her husband has died?

_____

10. What happens when Brently Mallard, Louise's husband, suddenly walks in the door?

_____

Answer Key

1. Gouvernail appears in "A Respectable Woman" and "Athénaïse."
2. At their plantation.
3. Mrs. Baroda is able to resist this impulse because she considers herself "a respectable woman."
4. Athénaïse's brother, Monteclin, helps her plot her escape.
5. Athénaïse stays in a boarding house of sorts in New Orleans.
6. While staying at the boarding house, Athénaïse develops a close platonic confidante-like friendship with a man, Gouvernail.
7. Athénaïse learns that she is pregnant.
8. Brently, Louise's husband, is supposed to have died in a train accident.
9. She initially weeps and is inconsolable, but soon feels a tremendous sense of freedom and possibility for her life now that she is free of her marriage.
10. Louise suffers a heart attack.

Day 4 - Crossword Puzzle

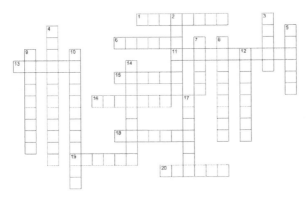

ACROSS

1. _____ comes to tell Louise Mallard of her husband's death
6. The name of the protagonist's husband in "A Respectable Woman"
11. Apprehension, dread, fear
13. Athénaïse's husband's name is _____
15. The French word for "pig"
16. Destructive or harmful
18. A small rivulet or creek
19. The owner of the New Orleans boarding house where Athénaïse stays
20. Gouvernail is a friend of Mr. _____'s

DOWN

2. Gouvernail is not interested in _____
3. Brently Mallard supposedly died in a _____ accident
4. Never-ending, endless
5. Household or domestic establishment
7. Louise suffers from a _____ condition
8. Modest, shy, unassuming
9. Vital, supremely important
10. With great disturbance or uproar
12. Sharpness, harshness, or abrasiveness
14. Who tries to comfort Louise in "The Story of an Hour"?
17. Monteclin is the _____ of Athénaïse

Crossword Puzzle Answer Key

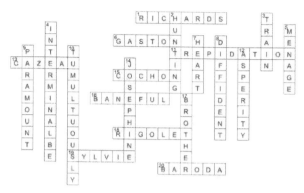

ACROSS

1. _____ comes to tell Louise Mallard of her husband's death
6. The name of the protagonist's husband in "A Respectable Woman"
11. Apprehension, dread, fear
13. Athénaïse's husband's name is _____
15. The French word for "pig"
16. Destructive or harmful
18. A small rivulet or creek
19. The owner of the New Orleans boarding house where Athénaïse stays
20. Gouvernail is a friend of Mr. _____'s

DOWN

2. Gouvernail is not interested in _____
3. Brently Mallard supposedly died in a _____ accident
4. Never-ending, endless
5. Household or domestic establishment
7. Louise suffers from a _____ condition
8. Modest, shy, unassuming
9. Vital, supremely important
10. With great disturbance or uproar
12. Sharpness, harshness, or abrasiveness
14. Who tries to comfort Louise in "The Story of an Hour"?
17. Monteclin is the _____ of Athénaïse

Day 4 - Vocabulary Quiz

Terms

1. _____ portico
2. _____ batture
3. _____ cravat
4. _____ apostrophe
5. _____ maudit
6. _____ dissimulation
7. _____ obsequiousness
8. _____ confab
9. _____ erudition
10. _____ elusive

Answers

A. pretense or deceit in showing one's thoughts, character, or feelings

B. hard to catch, find, or remember

C. the often rocky, damp area along the banks or in the middle of a river where the land rises out of the water at times and is submerged at other times

D. an informal, but usually private chat or discussion

E. a wide, short strip of fabric worn by men around the neck and tucked into the neck of a shirt; similar to a neck-tie

F. a structure with a roof supported by columns spaced regularly, often attached to a building (e.g. a wraparound porch)

G. the quality of showing deference or subservient complacence

H. a poet or bohemian living a life against or outside of society, often associated with someone who is an addict, criminal, or mentally unsound

I. a literary term meaning an address given by a speaker who has detached himself to reality and is speaking to an imaginary character or idea of some kind

J. possessing or demonstrating great knowledge, scholarship, or intellect

Answer Key

1. F portico: a structure with a roof supported by columns spaced regularly, often attached to a building (e.g. a wraparound porch)
2. C batture: the often rocky, damp area along the banks or in the middle of a river where the land rises out of the water at times and is submerged at other times
3. E cravat: a wide, short strip of fabric worn by men around the neck and tucked into the neck of a shirt; similar to a neck-tie
4. I apostrophe: a literary term meaning an address given by a speaker who has detached himself to reality and is speaking to an imaginary character or idea of some kind
5. H maudit: a poet or bohemian living a life against or outside of society, often associated with someone who is an addict, criminal, or mentally unsound
6. A dissimulation: pretense or deceit in showing one's thoughts, character, or feelings
7. G obsequiousness: the quality of showing deference or subservient complacence
8. D confab: an informal, but usually private chat or discussion
9. J erudition: possessing or demonstrating great knowledge, scholarship, or intellect
10. B elusive: hard to catch, find, or remember

Day 4 - Classroom Activities

1. Kate Chopin's Life and Times

Kind of Activity:

Long-term Project

Objective:

Students will be able to conduct research on life during the turn of the 20th century in the area around New Orleans and examine how societal changes may have impacted Chopin's life and writings.

Common Core Standards:

CCSS.ELA-Literacy.CCRA.R.4, CCSS.ELA-Literacy.CCRA.R.5, CCSS.ELA-Literacy.CCRA.SL.4

Time:

20-25 minutes (recurring)

Structure:

For an overview of this unit-long project, see the description in Day #1.

For Day #4, review the purpose of the activity and how it will continue through the unit. Then, demonstrate how to find important details from researching the world events and societal developments in America (and particularly the region around New Orleans) happening during Chopin's lifetime that could have impacted her perspectives about particular important themes in his writing. For example, identify the cultural shifts/themes that took place during the Reconstruction after The Civil War and the changes in women's rights at the beginning of the 20th century. Then identify a textual example of this theme arising in her writing. Next, check for understanding, asking students questions about the observations and inferences made about the selected theme. Then, depending on student understanding, lead students in a guided practice--identifying another societal or cultural event or aspect of Chopin's life and a textual example of a related theme--or proceed to splitting students into groups.

Again, have each group continue to research their assigned or selected theme. Again, themes might include: history of the New Orleans region; New Orleans "high society" culture during the turn of the 20th century; cultural expectations of women, marriage, and motherhood during this era; effects of Southern Reconstruction in the region during the late 19th and early 20th centuries; developments in women's rights during this time period; Chopin's Literary & Philosophical influences and contemporaries; Cultural/Religious Reactions to the women's rights movement, etc.

As in Days #1-3, the group scribe should chart the sociological events related to their group's theme, with a particular eye toward the ways that Day #4's readings have expanded their understanding of their assigned theme. Next, each group will examine the day's readings to find textual examples of the assigned theme. The group will then analyze their selected pieces of textual evidence and add them to their overall analysis.

Students will then share out one finding from their group with the whole class.

Ideas for Differentiated Instruction:

- Provide texts at a variety of reading levels depending on student ability.
- Provide some groups with the option to read aloud the biographical section, or listen to/watch audio or video pieces about Chopin as a form of research.
- Assign students different roles—scribe, head researcher, lead note-taker, presenter, etc.—based on skills or areas for growth.
- Split students into groups by skill-set or areas of need, so that some groups can work more independently, and the teacher can support other groups more.

Assessment Ideas:

- Student groups each generate a series of charts about an aspect of life or culture in Chopin's time and how it related to her writings, with specific references to *The Awakening* and Chopin's short stories.
- Student groups present findings from group chart to the rest of the class, while other students take notes in interactive handout on groups' presentations.
- Students complete a peer assessment of other group's presentations.

2. Making Creative Representations of Scenes from Kate Chopin's Writings

Kind of Activity:

Artistic Response

Objective:

Students will be able to represent a scene from Chopin's novel or stories in an alternative medium, and present their representation to the class.

Common Core Standards:

CCSS.ELA-Literacy.CCRA.R.7, CCSS.ELA-Literacy.CCRA.W.2

Time:

30-35 minutes

Structure:

Throughout *The Awakening* and the stories from Day 4's readings, Chopin uses extensive imagery and evocative metaphors, allowing the reader to truly envision and experience the complex social, cultural, and interpersonal themes she is trying to describe more concretely. In this activity, students will construct a creative representation of one of the scenes from *The Awakening* and Day 4's short stories, in whatever way they choose.

You can impose limitations on the types of media students are allowed to employ, or students can have free reign to choose whatever interpretation they want (e.g. dramatization or performance, painting, drawing, musical response, mural, audio-visual interpretation, poetic response, etc.). In addition, this project can be done in small groups or individually.

Explain the structure of the activity to students, giving an example of how one might choose to artistically represent a scene from what students have read so far in *The Awakening*. First, students should read their selected scene carefully and do an analysis of the text. Next, students should examine any notes or commentary on their selected scene and take notes on features or themes that they learn about. Then, students should create their own artistic interpretation of the selected scene in whatever medium they deem appropriate.

Finally, have students share or present their creative pieces to the class and discuss the process of re-interpreting a literary scene in a different medium.

Ideas for Differentiated Instruction:

- Depending on student independence, assign them to work as individuals or in small groups.
- Split students into groups by skill-set or areas of need, so that some groups can work more independently, and the teacher can support other groups more (e.g. participating in the student discussion, helping to make connections, etc.).
- Assign different students or groups different scenes to interpret, based on the scenes' levels of complexity.

Assessment Ideas:

- Students present or perform their artistic representation to the class and are assessed based on a rubric.
- Students offer feedback on other students' artistic representations, either in verbal or written form, perhaps through a class blog or Google site.
- Students write a 1-2 paragraph response about how their artistic representation relates to Chopin's original text.

3. The Woman in Question: Analyzing Themes in Kate Chopin's Private Papers

Kind of Activity:

Research

Objective:

Students will be able to conduct research and interpret primary source texts.

Common Core Standards:

CCSS.ELA-Literacy.CCRA.R.4, CCSS.ELA-Literacy.CCRA.R.5, CCSS.ELA-Literacy.CCRA.W.7, CCSS.ELA-Literacy.CCRA.W.8, CCSS.ELA-Literacy.CCRA.SL.4

Time:

40-45 minutes

Structure:

In this activity, students will be examining excerpts from Kate Chopin's private papers in small groups and relating them to themes identified in Chopin's stories that students have read thus far. The primary purpose is for students to be able to trace the connections between themes they've read about in Chopin's stories to events/ideas chronicled in the author's own personal papers.

Begin by reviewing the themes or recurring symbols discussed in class that have come up in different stories. This part can be done in small groups or led as a class-wide discussion. For the purposes of this activity, stick to themes and recurring symbols that play prominent roles in multiple stories, so that students have a number of places to look for textual connections.

After reviewing the notable themes and symbols covered so far, split students into small groups of 4-5 students and assign one theme/symbol to each group. Provide groups with selected sections from *Kate Chopin's Private Papers*, edited by Emily Toth and Per Seyersted (http://www.iupress.indiana.edu/product_info.php?products_id=19696), which includes a larger number of Chopin's previously unpublished letters, journal entries, unpublished story segments, etc. (or, for an added challenge, have students have to find their own references from the whole collection of Chopin's private papers).

Over the course of this activity, students should find 3-4 examples of their group's assigned theme/symbol (or related topics from which they can infer connections) in Chopin's private papers. Then, students should find 3-4 examples of their group's theme/symbol in the Chopin stories read so far. Finally, students will compile these thematic connections -- from both Chopin's private papers and her stories -- and present them to the class. This does not need to be a formal presentation necessarily, though it could be as an additional extension of this activity.

Ideas for Differentiated Instruction:

- Provide texts at a variety of reading levels depending on student ability.
- Provide students with the option to read aloud the biographical section, or listen to/watch audio or video pieces about Chopin as a form of research.
- Assign students different roles—scribe, head researcher, lead note-taker, presenter, etc.—based on skills or areas for growth.
- Split students into groups by skill-set or areas of need, so that some groups can work more independently, and the teacher can support other groups more.

Assessment Ideas:

- Student groups each generate a series of charts/shared documents about how their group's theme/symbol connects to Chopin's private papers and stories.
- Student groups present findings from group chart to the rest of the class, while other students take notes in interactive handout on other groups' theme presentations.
- Students complete a peer assessment of other group's presentations.

Day 5 - Reading Assignment, Questions, Vocabulary

Read "The Storm," "Désirée's Baby," and "A Pair of Silk Stockings"

Common Core Objectives

- CCSS.ELA-Literacy.CCRA.R.2--Determine central ideas or themes of a text and analyze their development; summarize the key supporting details and ideas.

- CCSS.ELA-Literacy.CCRA.R.3--Analyze how and why individuals, events, or ideas develop and interact over the course of a text.

- CCSS.ELA-Literacy.CCRA.R.4--Interpret words and phrases as they are used in a text, including determining technical, connotative, and figurative meanings, and analyze how specific word choices shape meaning or tone.

- CCSS.ELA-Literacy.CCRA.R.6--Assess how point of view or purpose shapes the content and style of a text.

- CCSS.ELA-Literacy.CCRA.W.3--Write narratives to develop real or imagined experiences or events using effective technique, well-chosen details and well-structured event sequences.

- CCSS.ELA-Literacy.CCRA.W.4--Produce clear and coherent writing in which the development, organization, and style are appropriate to task, purpose, and audience.

- CCSS.ELA-Literacy.CCRA.SL.1--Prepare for and participate effectively in a range of conversations and collaborations with diverse partners, building on others' ideas and expressing their own clearly and persuasively.

- CCSS.ELA-Literacy.CCRA.SL.3--Evaluate a speaker's point of view, reasoning, and use of evidence and rhetoric, identifying any fallacious reasoning or exaggerated or distorted evidence.

- CCSS.ELA-Literacy.CCRA.SL.4--Present information, findings, and supporting evidence such that listeners can follow the line of reasoning and the organization, development, and style are appropriate to task, purpose, and audience.

- CCSS.ELA-Literacy.CCRA.L.1--Demonstrate command of the conventions of standard English grammar and usage when writing or speaking.

- CCSS.ELA-Literacy.CCRA.L.5--Demonstrate understanding of figurative language, word relationships, and nuances in word meanings.

Note that it is perfectly fine to expand any day's work into two days depending on the characteristics of the class, particularly if the class will engage in all of the suggested classroom exercises and activities and discuss all of the thought questions.

Content Summary for Teachers

"The Storm"

Bobinôt and his four-year-old son, Bibi, are shopping at Friedheimer's store when a violent storm rolls in. The pair decide to wait until the storm passes to go home. While they wait, Bobinôt buys a can of shrimp for his wife, Calixta.

While her husband and son are out, Calixta has occupied herself with sewing back at the house, and she initially does not notice the storm approaching. She finally sees the ominous clouds rolling in and goes to shut the windows and get Bobinôt's clothes from outside. One of Calixta's former suitors, Alcée Labarille, rides up on his horse and helps her take down the clothes.

As the storm gets worse, Calixta invites Alcée inside to wait it out. Calixta worries about her husband and son, but Alcée tries to comfort her and reminisces about the attraction they once felt for each other. The storm gets more intense and the two rekindle their passion, but their sexual encounter ends with the storm, and Alcée leaves on his horse right after.

Calixta's husband and son return from the store, and she excitedly embraces them. Bobinôt gives the can of shrimp to his wife, and she is grateful, saying they will feast that night. At the same time, Alcée writes an affectionate letter to his wife, Clarisse, saying that she should stay on her trip to Biloxi as long as she wishes to for her health, although he says he does miss her. Clarisse appreciates Alcée's letter and enjoys her time in Biloxi, where she can feel again as if she is a maiden, free to do as she pleases. Though she loves her husband, Clarisse is happy to sacrifice intimacy for a while to extend her time away. The ending line reads, "so the storm passed and every one was happy."

"Désirée's Baby"

Madame Valmondé is visiting Désirée and her new baby in L'Abri; on her way there, she thinks back to when Désirée was a baby. Monsieur Valmondé had found Désirée as a baby asleep at the gate to their estate. Many people believed that a group of Texans passing through had left Désirée there, but Madame Valmondé thinks Providence brought this lovely, wonderful child to their doorstep since she didn't have her own children. When Désirée later meets and marries Armand Aubigny, he does not look into her lineage but simply gives her his last name.

Madame Valmondé has not been to visit Désirée and her baby for a month. When she arrives, she despairs at the lack of oversight of the Aubigny household. Madame Aubigny, Armand's mother, did not want to leave France, so no woman had ever fully taken over managing the estate. Armand is also a strict overseer of his slaves, so the easy-going nature of L'Abri has diminished over time.

When Madame Vamondé sees Désirée's baby, she is surprised at the infant's appearance. Désirée laughs and agrees that he has grown differently than expected. Madame Valmondé asks worriedly about Armand's thoughts, and Désirée explains that Armand is happy to have a son and that he has, in fact, softened his treatment towards his servants since the marriage and his son's birth. Armand's nature is to be demanding and domineering, but Désirée is desperately in love with him, and Armand has not had a bad day since they fell in love.

When Désirée's baby is three months old, she begins to feel a sense of menace and mystery in the air that troubles her, most notably marked by many unannounced visits and changes in Armand's behavior. One day, as she watches her son play, she glances at one of the slaves, a child with some black heritage, and sees a striking resemblance between him and her son. Désirée asks Armand what her observation means, and he harshly responds that if the child isn't fully white, she must not be fully white. Panicking, she responds that her appearance is clearly white--white skin, brown hair, and gray eyes. Armand coldly tells her that she is only as white as their mixed-race slave La Blanche. He leaves in anger.

Shocked and despairing at her husband's rejection, Désirée writes to Madame Valmondé to tell her what happened. Madame tells Désirée that she still loves her and to return to Valmondé with her baby. Désirée shows Armand the letter and he orders her to go. Without packing, Désirée takes her son and walks off, not to Valmondé but to a deserted area of the bayou. They disappear.

Several weeks later, Armand has his slaves at L'Abri feed a bonfire with the baby's cradle and other reminders of his marriage to Désirée and his mixed-race son. The final object Armand throws on the pyre is a bundle of letters, including one sent from Armand's mother to his father. Armand reads the letter, wherein his mother gives tthanks to God that Armand will never learn of her mixed-race heritage.

"A Pair of Silk Stockings"

Mrs. Sommers unexpectedly gets 15 dollars -- a large sum to her -- and it makes her feel momentarily wealthy and important. She thinks about how she should spend her money, feeling that she should determine a sensible use for it. After thinking about it,

Mrs. Sommers decides to spend a bit more on Janie's shoes so they will last longer, to purchase some cloth to make her children new garments, and to get everyone new hats and stockings. She is happy with this plan as her children haven't had new clothes in some time.

Mrs. Sommers had more money before her marriage, but she doesn't think about that time now, mainly focusing on the concerns of the present. While shopping, she impulsively buys a pair of two-dollar silk stockings -- an uncharacteristic break from her responsible penny-pinching. She also buys a fashionable pair of boots and gloves, as well as two pricey magazines that remind her of her past pleasures.

Feeling hungry, Mrs. Sommers continues to follow her impulses and goes out to eat, rather than waiting to get something at home. She has a small, delicious meal at a nice restaurant and leisurely drinks wine and reads her magazines. No one minds her presence and Mrs. Sommers does not worry about the cost, even leaving a tip on the way out. Next, Mrs. Sommers goes to the theater to see a play. While most of the audience is paying attention to the play, Mrs. Sommers is enraptured by the whole experience.

After the play, Mrs. Sommers gets on a cable car to go home. A man across from her in the car observes her expression, puzzled trying to figure out what on her mind. He doesn't see what Mrs. Sommers is really thinking -- that she wishes the cable car would not stop and instead would keep going on forever.

Thought Questions (students consider while they read)

1. Why do you think "The Storm" may not have been published during Kate Chopin's lifetime? (It was first published in *The Complete Works of Kate Chopin* in 1969)

2. What do you make of the final line of "The Storm"? ("So the storm passed and every one was happy"?)

3. Are you surprised by Armand's reaction to Désirée and her baby, once he sees how his son is beginning to look? Why or why not?

4. Why do you think Désirée walks off into the bayou in the middle of the night instead of going home to Madame Valmonté?

5. What is the significance of the metaphor that is initially used in discussing the stockings in "A Pair of Silk Stockings"? How do similar metaphors come up in *The Awakening* (and potentially Chopin's other stories)?

Vocabulary (in order of appearance)

"It shook the wooden store and seemed to be ripping great furrows in the distant field." (The Storm)

furrow:

rut or trench, often made by a plow

"She unfastened her white sacque at the throat." (The Storm)

sacque:

a short, fashionable jacket that buttons at the neck

"...there were plows and a harrow piled up in the corner." (The Storm)

harrow:

an agricultural implement used for plowing multiple rows in the soil at once

"It was stiflingly hot." (The Storm)

stiflingly:

overwhelmingly, crushingly, oppressively

"If she was not an immaculate dove in those days, she was still inviolate..." (The Storm)

inviolate:

safe from violation, untouchable

"He stayed cushioned upon her, breathless, dazed, enervated, with his heart beating like a hammer upon her." (The Storm)

enervated:

fatigued, exhausted

"He scraped the mud off Bibi's bare legs and feet with a stick and carefully removed all traces from his heavy brogans." (The Storm)

brogans:

short, stout leather ankle boots or shoes

"Devoted as she was to her husband, their intimate conjugal life was something which she was more than willing to forego for a while." (The Storm)

conjugal:

related to marriage or the affairs of a married couple

"'I knew you would be astonished,' laughed Désirée, 'at the way he has grown. The little cochon de lait!...'" (Désirée's Baby)

cochon de lait:

a French Creole term for a young, suckling pig (a term of endearment)

"Désirée's face became suffused with a glow that was happiness itself." (Désirée's Baby)

suffused:

covered, permeated, bathed

"What Désirée said was true. Marriage, and later the birth of his son had softened Armand Aubigny's imperious and exacting nature greatly." (Désirée's Baby)

imperious:

high-handed, domineering, arrogantly commanding

exacting:

stringent, demanding, arduously precise

"A quick conception of all that this accusation meant for her nerved her with unwonted courage to deny it." (Désirée's Baby)

unwonted:

unusual, atypical

"Désirée went in search of her child. Zandrine was pacing the sombre gallery with it." (Désirée's Baby)

sombre:

drab, dark, gloomy

"A graceful cradle of willow, with all its dainty furbishings, was laid upon the pyre, which had already been fed with the richness of a priceless layette." (Désirée's Baby)

layette:

a newborn baby's set of toiletries, clothes, and linens

"Then there were silk gowns, and velvet and satin ones added to these; laces, too, and embroideries; bonnets and gloves; for the corbeille had been of rare quality." (Désirée's Baby)

corbeille:

an elegant basket of fruit, flowers, etc., like cornucopia

"...she seemed to see her way clearly toward a proper and judicious use of the money." (A Pair of Silk Stockings)

judicious:

prudent, wise, sensible, showing good judgement

"She was fastidious. The clerk could not make her out; he could not reconcile her shoes with her stockings, and she was not too easily pleased." (A Pair of Silk Stockings)

fastidious:

very attentive to detail, painstaking, meticulous

"In truth, he saw nothing—unless he were wizard enough to detect a poignant wish, a powerful longing that the cable car would never stop anywhere, but go on and on with her forever." (A Pair of Silk Stockings)

poignant:

touching or moving in a sad or sentimental way

Additional Homework

1. Watch the PBS documentary "Kate Chopin: A Re-Awakening" (more information available here) and write a 1-2 page review of the program.

Day 5 - Discussion of Thought Questions

1. Why do you think "The Storm" may not have been published during Kate Chopin's lifetime? (It was first published in *The Complete Works of Kate Chopin* in 1969)

Time:

5-7 minutes

Discussion:

Students may not know a lot about the specifics of women's magazines or how publishing and content censorship worked during Chopin's time, but they could infer some of this from the research they've been doing in the "Kate Chopin's Life and Times" classroom activity. At the time when Kate Chopin wrote this story, the content would've been considered far too risqué for any respectable American magazine to publish. Even more progressive and open-minded magazines, such as Vogue, where Chopin published many stories, would not have touched something this sexually explicit. It seems that Chopin probably knew this reality, as there is no evidence that she sent it out to publishers when she wrote it or at all during her lifetime; in fact it was not published at all until *The Complete Works of Kate Chopin* came out in 1969.

2. What do you make of the final line of "The Storm"? ("So the storm passed and every one was happy"?)

Time:

8-10 minutes

Discussion:

Since this question couples students' personal opinions about and understandings of the characters's mental states with textual analysis, students may have all different kinds of reactions to the ending of the story.

Students might think that the final line means that, as long as the "storm" of passion is only temporary, it does not impact one's normal life. Others may argue that the concept being discussed here is broader and relates more to concepts of the complacency of marriage as compared to the furor of illicit passion. Perhaps Chopin's point here is that a storm of that kind of passion couldn't continue forever, because it is so tumultuous.

3. Are you surprised by Armand's reaction to Désirée and her baby, once he sees how his son is beginning to look? Why or why not?

Time:

5-7 minutes

Discussion:

Some students may have been surprised by Armand's severe reaction to his wife's supposed lineage, especially since he seems at first to be a doting husband and Désirée is very much in love with him. However by this point in the unit, students should have done significant research about race relations, class divides, and related cultural norms during Chopin's time, which could help them understand the import of Armand and Désirée's realization about their son.

There is also some foreshadowing earlier in the story that suggests that Armand Aubigny is not a particularly kind man. Désirée also makes an odd comment when Madame Valmondé asks her about Armand's opinion on the baby. Désirée explains that Armand is happy to have a son and that he has, in fact, softened his treatment towards his servants since the marriage and his son's birth. Armand's nature is to be demanding and domineering, so when he is cruel towards Désirée once he finds out about what he believes to be her secret heritage, he simply demonstrates again that his supposed love for her was built on very shaky ground.

4. Why do you think Désirée walks off into the bayou in the middle of the night instead of going home to Madame Valmonté?

Time:

5-7 minutes

Discussion:

The ending of "Désirée's Baby" is one of Chopin's most famous and provocative, and students might have strong opinions about why Désirée chooses to do what she does and whether she is justified in doing so. Some students may be appalled that Désirée would do such a thing to her own child or may assume that she was somewhat insane or unstable herself in some way. Other students might be more sympathetic to her unstated but still clear belief that she and her son would be rejected the world over. Perhaps in Désirée's eyes, she saw her husband's rejection of her as symbolic of the society rejecting her -- which, at the time, it would have for the most part. Even if Madame Valmondé still loved her and was willing to take her and her grand-son in, perhaps Désirée felt that she would never be able to actually live a normal life, nor would her son, because of their mixed blood. At the time when this story is set, Désirée was actually probably correct in many respects, and her decision to take her own life might have been seen as the ultimate maternal sacrifice for her son, rather than an insane murder-suicide by a grief-stricken woman.

5. What is the significance of the metaphor that is initially used in discussing the stockings in "A Pair of Silk Stockings"? How do similar metaphors come up in *The Awakening (*and potentially Chopin's other stories)?

Time:

8-10 minutes

Discussion:

When Mrs. Sommers initially goes shopping with the intent of making practical purchases, she gets tempted into indulging her own material desires by touching a pair of silk stockings. She is described "holding [the stockings] up to see them glisten, and to feel them glide serpent-like through her fingers." This "serpent-like" metaphor is a biblical reference to the story of Adam and Eve getting tempted by the serpent (Satan) in the Garden of Eden. The reference might represent the temptation of material wealth and luxury, or it might have a broader meaning of Mrs. Sommers giving in to her self-interested desires, rather than always trying to please and be responsible for everyone else in her family.

A similar reference came up in *The Awakening* during the childbirth scene with Madame Ratignolle. In this scene, Madame Ratignolle's hair is braided down and lies "coiled like a golden serpent" on the sofa beside her. In this moment, Madame Ratignolle shows the dark side of the human condition, revealing it to be full of pain and turmoil, even with the comforts afforded to the social elite. In addition, Madame Ratignolle's inability to maintain her motherly serenity in this torturous moment reveals to Edna the futility of romanticizing life and the world. By repeating this metaphor in these different contexts, Chopin may be trying to demonstrate the various ways society's expectations of women's behavior, desires, and needs does not necessarily fit with the realities of being a woman, wife, and mother.

Day 5 - Short Answer Evaluation

1. What does Bobinôt purchase for his wife when he's stuck at the store during the storm?

   _____

2. Who is Alcée in "The Storm"?

   _____

3. In "The Storm," where is Alcée's wife, Clarisse?

   _____

4. In "Désirée's Baby," who or what does Madame Valmondé think brought her daughter, Désirée, to her?

   _____

5. What is Madame Valmondé's reaction when she sees Désirée's baby again after a month of being apart?

   _____

6. What events around the house begin to make Désirée feel a sense of foreboding around when the baby turns 3-months-old?

   _____

7. In "Désirée's Baby," who is La Blanche?

   _____

8. What is revealed in the old letter Armand reads from his mother to his father?

9. In "A Pair of Silk Stockings," what items does Mrs. Sommers buy on her shopping trip?

10. How does Mrs. Sommers feel when she is on the cable car going home?

Answer Key

1. Bobinôt buys Calixta a can of shrimp.
2. Alcée is one of Calixta's old suitors who stops by as the storm begins.
3. She is visiting Biloxi.
4. Madame Valmondé believed that Providence brought Désirée to her.
5. Madame Valmondé is alarmed at the changed appearance of the infant.
6. Désirée feels a general sense of menace approaching, but seems most troubled by the mysterious, unannounced visits from neighbors they've had recently and the odd changes in Armand's behavior.
7. La Blanche is the light-skinned slave who Armand cruelly equates his wife, Désirée, with when he believes she is part-black.
8. He learns that his mother was half-black.
9. Mrs. Sommers buys black silk stockings, boots, gloves, magazines, all for herself, and also takes herself to a nice dinner and to the theater.
10. She wishes the cable car would not stop and instead would keep going on forever.

Day 5 - Crossword Puzzle

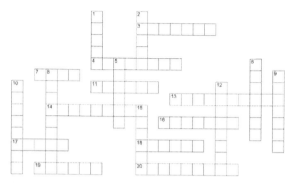

ACROSS

3. Armand surname in "Désirée's Baby"
4. Covered, permeated, bathed
7. The name of Calixta's young son.
11. Bobinôt buys _____ for his wife, Calixta
13. Overwhelmingly, crushingly, oppressively
14. High-handed, domineering, arrogantly commanding
16. In "A Pair of Silk Stockings," Mrs. _____ goes shopping
17. Many suspect Désirée was orphaned by a band of vagabonds from _____
18. Where is Alcée's wife currently visiting in "The Storm"?
19. What is Calixta doing before the storm begins?
20. Fatigued, exhausted

DOWN

1. After buying stockings, what does the protagonist buy next?
2. Where does Désirée disappear with her son?
5. Rut or trench, often made by a plow
6. Short, stout leather ankle boots or shoes
8. Safe from violation, untouchable
9. A newborn baby's set of toiletries, clothes, and linens
10. Unusual, atypical
12. Alcée's wife is named _____
15. Drab, dark, gloomy (British spelling)

Crossword Puzzle Answer Key

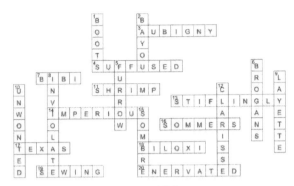

ACROSS

3. Armand surname in "Désirée's Baby"
4. Covered, permeated, bathed
7. The name of Calixta's young son.
11. Bobinôt buys _____ for his wife, Calixta
13. Overwhelmingly, crushingly, oppressively
14. High-handed, domineering, arrogantly commanding
16. In "A Pair of Silk Stockings," Mrs. _____ goes shopping
17. Many suspect Désirée was orphaned by a band of vagabonds from _____
18. Where is Alcée's wife currently visiting in "The Storm"?
19. What is Calixta doing before the storm begins?
20. Fatigued, exhausted

DOWN

1. After buying stockings, what does the protagonist buy next?
2. Where does Désirée disappear with her son?
5. Rut or trench, often made by a plow
6. Short, stout leather ankle boots or shoes
8. Safe from violation, untouchable
9. A newborn baby's set of toiletries, clothes, and linens
10. Unusual, atypical
12. Alcée's wife is named _____
15. Drab, dark, gloomy (British spelling)

Day 5 - Vocabulary Quiz

Terms

1. _____ sacque
2. _____ harrow
3. _____ conjugal
4. _____ cochon de lait
5. _____ imperious
6. _____ exacting
7. _____ corbeille
8. _____ judicious
9. _____ fastidious
10. _____ poignant

Answers

A. related to marriage or the affairs of a married couple

B. an agricultural implement used for plowing multiple rows in the soil at once

C. touching or moving in a sad or sentimental way

D. high-handed, domineering, arrogantly commanding

E. a French Creole term for a young, suckling pig (a term of endearment)

F. a short, fashionable jacket that buttons at the neck

G. stringent, demanding, arduously precise

H. prudent, wise, sensible, showing good judgement

I. very attentive to detail, painstaking, meticulous

J. an elegant basket of fruit, flowers, etc., like cornucopia

Answer Key

1. F sacque: a short, fashionable jacket that buttons at the neck
2. B harrow: an agricultural implement used for plowing multiple rows in the soil at once
3. A conjugal: related to marriage or the affairs of a married couple
4. E cochon de lait: a French Creole term for a young, suckling pig (a term of endearment)
5. D imperious: high-handed, domineering, arrogantly commanding
6. G exacting: stringent, demanding, arduously precise
7. J corbeille: an elegant basket of fruit, flowers, etc., like cornucopia
8. H judicious: prudent, wise, sensible, showing good judgement
9. I fastidious: very attentive to detail, painstaking, meticulous
10. C poignant: touching or moving in a sad or sentimental way

Day 5 - Classroom Activities

1. Kate Chopin's Life and Times

Kind of Activity:

Long-term Project

Objective:

Students will be able to conduct research on life during the turn of the 20th century in the area around New Orleans and examine how societal changes may have impacted Chopin's life and writings.

Common Core Standards:

CCSS.ELA-Literacy.CCRA.R.4, CCSS.ELA-Literacy.CCRA.R.5, CCSS.ELA-Literacy.CCRA.W.7, CCSS.ELA-Literacy.CCRA.W.8, CCSS.ELA-Literacy.CCRA.SL.4

Time:

20-25 minutes (recurring)

Structure:

For an overview of this unit-long project, see the description in Day #1.

For Day #5, if needed, review the purpose of the activity by reviewing how it will work and how it will continue through the unit. An overview of these review steps can be found in the Day #1-Day #4 descriptions of this activity's structure. These review steps can be skipped if they are unnecessary for your class at this stage.

In addition, for Day #5, introduce the expectations and stipulations for the final group presentation/project related to this activity. This presentation/project could take any form--digital/multimedia presentation, posters, performance, paper, etc.--but should include both evidence of a thorough and in-depth research in to the group's assigned theme, as well as in-depth analysis of at least 5 of the *Awakening* or short stories scenes studied in this unit. At this stage of this unit-long group project, groups should finalize the planning and development of their group presentation/project, so that it can be presented or submitted at the end of the unit.

After explaining the next steps related to the final presentation/project, as in previous days of this activity, have each group continue to research their assigned or selected theme. Again, themes might include: history of the New Orleans region; New Orleans "high society" culture during the turn of the 20th century; cultural expectations of women, marriage, and motherhood during this era; effects of Southern Reconstruction in the region during the late 19th and early 20th centuries; developments in women's rights during this time period; Chopin's Literary & Philosophical influences and contemporaries; Cultural/Religious Reactions to the women's rights movement, etc.

As in Days #1-4, the group scribe should chart the sociological events related to their group's theme, with a particular eye toward the ways that Day #5's readings have expanded their understanding of their assigned theme. Next, each group will examine the day's readings to find textual examples of the assigned theme. The group will then analyze their selected pieces of textual evidence and add them to their overall analysis.

Finally, as in previous days, students will then share out one finding from their group with the whole class.

Ideas for Differentiated Instruction:

- Provide texts at a variety of reading levels depending on student ability.
- Provide some groups with the option to read aloud the biographical section, or listen to/watch audio or video pieces about Chopin as a form of research.
- Assign students different roles—scribe, head researcher, lead note-taker, presenter, etc.—based on skills or areas for growth.
- Split students into groups by skill-set or areas of need, so that some groups can work more independently, and the teacher can support other groups more.

Assessment Ideas:

- Student groups each generate a series of charts about an aspect of life or culture in Chopin's time and how it related to her writings, with specific references to *The Awakening* and Chopin's short stories.
- Students present findings from group chart to the rest of the class.
- Students take notes, using an interactive handout (digital or paper), on other groups' theme presentations.
- Students present overall research and analysis at end of unit, using multimedia (audio/video/picture) presentations.

2. Surprise Scene Workshop: Creating Your Own Chopin Scene

Kind of Activity:

Creative Writing

Objective:

Students will be able to evaluate Chopin's use of imagery and symbolism to convey larger themes, write their own scene using selected symbols and themes.

Common Core Standards:

CCSS.ELA-Literacy.CCRA.R.3, CCSS.ELA-Literacy.CCRA.W.3

Time:

40-45 minutes

Structure:

In this activity, students will have to write an additional "bonus" scene for *The Awakening* or any of the other stories read in this unit, using randomly selected themes and symbols (one of each, and based on those used by Chopin). To introduce the activity, explain the way in which Chopin often uses unique symbols and imagery to discuss and explain much larger societal and existential concepts. Explain that, now that the class is more familiar with Chopin's style and the overall plot and characters in her stories, they are going to write their own creative scenes using Chopin's symbolism, imagery, and thematic styles themselves.

Show how students will participate in this activity by randomly selecting a theme and a symbol, brainstorming briefly about how to correlate the theme to the symbol. Then demonstrate writing the first paragraph or so of a scene. Make sure to note for students that, while the symbol they select should play a primary role in their scene, it does not have to be the only symbol they use and can be incorporated into a larger extended metaphor--this will give students more flexibility and options for expressing themselves, while keeping the complexity of instructions to a minimum. In addition, tell students that their scene must be at least 2 pages (no maximum), must include at least 2 characters from the novel, and does not necessarily need to be written with the structure and form of Chopin's style.

Next, have students pick one theme and one symbol at random (e.g. write them on slips of paper in two separate bowls and have students pick them, or hand cards out to students randomly). Then, have the class get to writing.

After students have finished writing, have students read their scenes to a partner or small group and explain how they chose to combine their symbol and theme in writing the scene. Alternatively, ask 1-2 students to share their scenes aloud and explain their creative choices to the class as a whole.

Ideas for Differentiated Instruction:

- Select specific students to read their scenes aloud, based on reading level and comfort with public reading.
- Provide some students with sentence starters or leading questions to help them understand and interpret their selected theme and symbol.
- This activity could also be done in small groups to facilitate different students' skills and writing abilities. In addition, this writing project could be continued as an at-home project if students are unable to finish it in the time allotted.

Assessment Ideas:

- Give students the opportunity to provide feedback on their peers' scenes and fill out an evaluation rubric.
- Have students turn in their scenes for teacher assessment or editing.
- Ask students to write 1-2 paragraphs reflecting on the process of writing the scene, and why they chose to combine their selected symbol and theme as they did.

3. The Critics Debate: For and Against Kate Chopin & Her Writing

Kind of Activity:

Group Work

Objective:

Students will be able to analyze the critical responses to Kate Chopin's work during and after her lifetime.

Common Core Standards:

CCSS.ELA-Literacy.CCRA.R.2, CCSS.ELA-Literacy.CCRA.R.4, CCSS.ELA-Literacy.CCRA.W.3, CCSS.ELA-Literacy.CCRA.SL.2

Time:

50-60 minutes (could be split into 2 separate 25-30 minute parts on different days)

Structure:

In this activity, students will examine the critical responses to Kate Chopin and her writing, both when she originally published it and since her death, and examine the cultural norms and expectations that underlay some of the critical reception and controversy surround Chopin's work. Next, students will split into two teams to debate the value and importance of Chopin's writing, from the perspectives of Chopin's contemporaries, one side arguing "for" Chopin and her writing and the other "against."

First, provide students with a variety of research stations where they can explore the different kinds of popular and literary criticism that has been written about Kate Chopin and her writing, both during her lifetime and since her works were re-popularized in the middle of the 20th century. Provide students with guided worksheets or instruct them to independently take notes on the different resources provided. Alternatively, students could do this research in small groups in order to facilitate more discussion and support for students who may be unsure how to evaluate primary source documents independently.

While there is a wide variety of excellent scholarship available about Kate Chopin's writing from modern perspectives available on the internet, make sure to either pre-select resources for students to examine or ensure they know how to assess the quality of literary analyses found online. In addition, students should analyze several critical responses by Kate Chopin's contemporaries, examining the connections between cultural expectations of the time and Kate's writings. Although students can conduct their own independent research as well, these links will provide an excellent jumping off point:

- http://www.ipl.org/div/litcrit/bin/litcrit.out.pl?au=cho-30
- http://people.virginia.edu/~sfr/enlt255/awcrit.html
- http://www.literaryhistory.com/19thC/Chopin.htm
- http://jottedlines.com/literature/critical-analysis-of-the-storm-by-kate-chopin/
- http://www.womenwriters.net/domesticgoddess/sprinkle.htm
- http://www.katechopin.org/faq/
- http://www.loyno.edu/~bewell/

- http://edsitement.neh.gov/lesson-plan/kate-chopins-awakening-no-choice-under#sect-activities
- http://www.womenwriters.net/domesticgoddess/chopin1.htm
- http://www.people.virginia.edu/~sfr/enlt255/awakeningnow.html

Then, after students have examined both the criticisms of Kate Chopin and her writing by her contemporaries, as well as defenses from both her lifetime and modern-day, split students into two debate teams-- one "for" the value and importance of Kate Chopin's work and the other "against." Then, have students begin to work with their team to develop 3-4 different arguments in defense of their team's position, incorporating examples from critical texts, as well as from Chopin's own writings. Although there should ultimately be two teams debating, the teams could be divided into more student groups to collaboratively write the different arguments.

Both teams should attempt to argue from the perspective of Chopin's contemporaries as much as possible, incorporating the kinds of themes, references, language, and cultural norms they would be accustomed to. Students can, however, use modern information about Kate Chopin's life or writings that her contemporaries may not have known, as we as incorporating analysis from modern-day critics and Chopin scholars.

After teams have had sufficient time to develop their arguments, conduct an actual debate in which students respond to each others arguments both with their prepared remarks (as well as impromptu responses, if desired).

Ideas for Differentiated Instruction:

- Select students for groups, teams, or roles based on skills or areas for growth; give other students with different skills or areas for growth different ways of demonstrating understanding and engagement.
- Provide various levels of scaffolding in the worksheets and charts distributed to students—some can have additional questions or sentence starters to get students thinking about the right themes, others can have challenge or in-depth thinking questions
- Provide students with various multimedia options for exploring the popular and literary criticisms of Kate Chopin and her work, if needed (e.g. watching videos, online presentations, etc.)

Assessment Ideas:

- Students individually complete graphic organizers or note-taking templates and submit for feedback.
- Evaluate students based on their participation in the research and writing activities and the debate, as well as the quality of the arguments their groups/teams present.

Final Paper

Essay Questions

1. Examine the last chapter of *The Awakening* and write a 2-3 page analysis of the ending. Then, write a 3-4 page epilogue for the novel from the perspective of one of the main characters.

2. Select one character in *The Awakening* and one character in any of the other Chopin short stories read in this unit, and compare and contrast how these two characters approach and understand one of the themes or symbols that arise in both works.

3. For this more creatively-oriented project, select one or more chapters from *The Awakening* or the entirety of one of Chopin's other stories, examine the events and imagery in the selected scenes, and then create a storyboard or comic book of the imagery and events in the scene(s). In addition to creating the storyboard or comic book, write a 2-page reflection of the scene(s) selected and how you chose to represent them visually.

4. Choose one of the chapter in *The Awakening* and re-write it from the perspective of a particular character. Make sure to consider the unique voices, beliefs, and prejudices seen in both the original, omniscient, perspective of the scene, as well as those of the new scene narrator, and reflect those differences in your re-envisioning of the chapter.

5. How does Chopin explore the themes of Love, Sexual Desire, and Sensual Experience in different ways over the course of *The Awakening* and the other short stories from this unit? Examine how Chopin uses this theme throughout these stories to communicate different ideas about the characters and the world more broadly.

6. Based on your understanding of the tension between women's traditional roles as wife and mother and the burgeoning women's rights movement of Chopin's time, write an analytical research paper about the way in which *The Awakening* and any other two of Chopin's stories expresses the cultural shifts taking place in American culture at the time. Use external sources to support your arguments about historical and cultural context.

7. How does Chopin use various kinds of water symbolically in different ways over the course of *The Awakening* and 1-2 other short stories studied in this unit? Compare and contrast how these symbols are used in different contexts throughout the novel and stories to communicate different ideas about the primary characters.

Advice on research sources

A. School or community library -- Ask your reference librarian for help locating books on the following subjects:

- Kate Chopin and her biography
- Chopin's stories and other writings
- Late 19th and early 20th century American literature by women
- The late 19th and early 20th century in the New Orleans region, and associated social and societal changes in the American South and New Orleans culture
- French Creole & New Orleans-area literature, philosophies, and values
- Women's issues and race relations in the late-19th and early-20th century New Orleans region
- Authors influencing and influenced by Chopin

B. Internet research

New Orleans regional history:

- http://www.history.com/topics/new-orleans
- http://www.neworleansonline.com/neworleans/history/
- http://www.louisianafolklife.org/LT/Articles_Essays/ creole_art_creole_state.html
- http://www.neworleansonline.com/neworleans/multicultural/ multiculturalhistory/french.html
- http://www.museumofthecity.org/project/african-american-culture-in-new-orleans/
- http://www.neworleansonline.com/neworleans/multicultural/ multiculturalhistory/creole.html

Kate Chopin's life and writing:

- http://www.katechopin.org/
- https://americanliterature.com/author/kate-chopin/bio-books-stories
- http://www.pbs.org/katechopin/
- http://archive.vcu.edu/english/engweb/webtexts/hour/katebio.html
- http://docsouth.unc.edu/southlit/chopinawake/bio.html
- http://classiclit.about.com/library/bl-bio/bl-kchopin.htm

The Awakening and Kate Chopin's short stories - analysis:

- http://www.gradesaver.com/the-awakening
- http://www.litcharts.com/lit/the-awakening
- https://jwpblog.files.wordpress.com/2012/01/chopin-study-guide.pdf
- https://muse.jhu.edu/article/31709

- http://www.inquiriesjournal.com/articles/657/kate-chopins-the-awakening-struggle-against-society-and-nature
- http://www.katechopin.org/the-awakening/

Developments in Women's Rights & Societal Role at the turn of the 20th century:

- http://www.gilderlehrman.org/history-by-era/womens-history/essays/women-american-politics-twentieth-century
- http://history.house.gov/Exhibitions-and-Publications/WIC/Historical-Essays/No-Lady/Womens-Rights/
- http://study.com/academy/lesson/feminism-in-the-19th-century-womens-rights-roles-and-limits.html
- https://www.nwhm.org/online-exhibits/progressiveera/suffrage.html
- http://www.enotes.com/topics/feminism/critical-essays/women-early-mid-20th-century-1900-1960
- http://www.loyno.edu/~kchopin/new/women/motherhood.html
- http://www.writereaderteacher.com/2013/06/gender-roles-in-late-1800s-and-early.html
- http://www.gilderlehrman.org/history-by-era/jackson-lincoln/essays/women-and-early-industrial-revolution-united-states

C. Personal experience

- What do you think about the importance of class and social status differences?
- What roles do class, social justice issues, and societal expectations play in your life?
- What role do societal expectations, based on your gender, race, or background, play in your life?
- What are your perspectives on marriage, children, women's rights, independence and free will, social obligation, and pursuing one's own desires at the expense of others?
- Consider how Chopin's life experiences may have impacted her worldview and the perspectives portrayed in her writings, drawing upon examples in your own life of how your experiences have affected their outlooks about certain topics.

Grading rubric for essays

Style:

- words: spelling and diction
- sentences: grammar and punctuation
- paragraphs: organization
- essay: structure
- argument: rhetoric, reasonableness, creativity

Content:

- accuracy
- use of evidence
- use of research as appropriate
- addresses the question
- completeness
- uses literary concepts

Answer Key for Final Essays

Remember that essays about literature should not be graded with a cookie-cutter approach whereby specific words or ideas are required. See the grading rubric above for a variety of criteria to use in assessing answers to the essay questions. This answer key thus functions as a store of ideas for students who need additional guidance in framing their answers.

1. Examine the last chapter of *The Awakening* and write a 2-3 page analysis of the ending. Then, write a 3-4 page epilogue for the novel from the perspective of one of the main characters.

For the first part of this topic, a strong paper will include evidence of a close-reading of the final chapter of the novel, as indicated by multiple specific and well-thought-out textual references, coupled with an evaluation that addresses some or all of the following questions: Does the student think the ending was compelling? Effective? What was the final message? What had been learned or achieved at the end of the novel? What can the reader take away from the novel relating to women's rights and independence, the realities of matrimony and motherhood, female sexuality, and the concept of free will? How does this ending impact other people in Edna's life? Is her suicide a final act of defiance or a way of allowing her family to be free of her? Could it be both?

For the second part of this paper topic, students must write an epilogue to the novel from one of the main character's perspectives (or from the perspective of the semi-omniscient narrator in the rest of the novel). High-quality pieces for this section should incorporate some of the themes, symbols, and ideas found in the rest of the novel. Furthermore, the best pieces will strive to mimic Chopin's tone and voice from the rest of the novel.

2. Select one character in *The Awakening* and one character in any of the other Chopin short stories read in this unit, and compare and contrast how these two

characters approach and understand one of the themes or symbols that arise in both works.

Strong responses will include evidence of a close-reading of multiple specific and well-thought-out textual references, coupled with an evaluation of what these references suggest about the characters and how their unique voices develop the narrative. In addition, strong answers will clearly identify the subject matter, themes, or symbols the two characters contrast, and will select 1 focus theme or symbol to compare and contrast between the two characters' perspectives.

Finally, depending on the length of the essay, the strongest responses will include either a brief examination of how cultural and ideological debates in Chopin's time might relate to the comparative approaches the two characters take to their selected theme or symbol, or how these characters approaches to the subject matter relate to other characters' beliefs and ideologies in *The Awakening* or other Chopin stories from this unit.

3. For this more creatively-oriented project, select one or more chapters from *The Awakening* or the entirety of one of Chopin's other stories, examine the events and imagery in the selected scenes, and then create a storyboard or comic book of the imagery and events in the scene(s). In addition to creating the storyboard or comic book, write a 2-page reflection of the scene(s) selected and how you chose to represent them visually.

Due to the open-ended nature of this project, students could create a storyboard or comic book out of almost any of the series of scenes in any of Chopin's stories read in this unit. The project itself should be graded on the following criteria:

- Are the chapters/scenes chosen part of a coherent section of the novel/ story?
- Does the student's visual representation properly reflect the events in the chapters/scenes selected?
- Does the imagery used in the storyboard/comic book reflect a solid understanding of the metaphors, themes, and symbols in the selected section?
- Do the storyboard/comic book scenes have the same ultimate meaning and impact on the reader as the scene as written by Chopin?

For the essay portion of this topic, students could supply many possible well-supported and thoughtful answers. A strong response should include a clear and thorough explanation of the process of creating the storyboard/comic book. In addition, students should provide evidence of a close-analysis of 2-3 of the specific artistic choices they made in their projects and how these choices reflect their interpretations of the chapters/scenes. These examples should include multiple specific and well thought out textual references, coupled with an evaluation of what these instances suggest about the underlying meaning of the selected chapters/scenes.

4. Choose one of the chapter in *The Awakening* and re-write it from the perspective of a particular character. Make sure to consider the unique voices, beliefs, and prejudices seen in both the original, omniscient, perspective of the scene, as well as those of the new scene narrator, and reflect those differences in your re-envisioning of the chapter.

Strong responses will include evidence of close-readings of the selected scene, demonstrated by insightful and relevant re-envisionings of the scene from the new character's perspective. In addition, strong answers will clearly identify the subject matter, themes, and symbols at play in the new interpretation of the scene. For example, students re-write the chapter in which Edna swims for the first time out into the ocean on her own from her husband, Léonce's, perspective.

Students should also make sure to consider the unique voices, beliefs, and prejudices of both the original focus character of the chapter, as well as the new focus character, and reflect those differences in their re-writes of the chapter. Finally, depending on the length of the essay, the best responses will include the new narrator of the scene interacting with other characters in the novel, in order to demonstrate larger ideas that arise in the novel, outside of the one chapter they are re-writing.

5. How does Chopin explore the themes of Love, Sexual Desire, and Sensual Experience in different ways over the course of *The Awakening* and the other short stories from this unit? Examine how Chopin uses this theme throughout these stories to communicate different ideas about the characters and the world more broadly.

Many of the protagonists in Chopin's stories find themselves confronted with sensual experiences that make them think of both love and sexual desire in new ways. These sensual experiences that tap into their physical desires often inspire the protagonists to pursue more freedom, independence, and personal experiences. Strong responses will recognize this connection to another crucial theme in Chopin's work: Freedom and Independence.

Most of the stories read in this unit -- in particular *The Awakening*, "A Respectable Woman," "Athénaïse," "The Story of an Hour," and "A Pair of Silk Stockings" -- feature women who must choose between fulfilling their duties to their husbands and children, and pursuing their own independent desires. They often realize or remember they have these personal wishes and wants once those desires are sparked by a sensual experience of some sort. Strong responses should include evidence of a close-reading of at least 1-2 different examples of the thematic role of love, sexual desire, and/or sensual experience in *The Awakening* and the same number of examples from at least one other short story.

6. Based on your understanding of the tension between women's traditional roles as wife and mother and the burgeoning women's rights movement of Chopin's time, write an analytical research paper about the way in which *The Awakening* and any other two of Chopin's stories expresses the cultural shifts taking place in American culture at the time. Use external sources to support your arguments about historical and cultural context.

Strong answers will include 2-3 different textual examples each from *The Awakening* and the two other stories that demonstrate how Chopin incorporates and thinks about women's issues and the related societal/ideological tensions in her era. These examples should be carefully selected and analyzed in the context of Chopin's historical framework.

Students should also include carefully chosen explanations of relevant women's rights issues and other sociological changes taking place in American, and specifically New Orleans, society in late 19th and early 20th century. In addition, the best responses will incorporate an examination of how Chopin's life events might relate to the role of women's-issues-related themes in her writing.

7. How does Chopin use various kinds of water symbolically in different ways over the course of *The Awakening* and <u>1-2</u> other short stories studied in this unit? Compare and contrast how these symbols are used in different contexts throughout the novel and stories to communicate different ideas about the primary characters.

Water plays an important role in various ways across several different stories. The sea, of course, plays a crucial role throughout *The Awakening*, and rain is pivotal component of the story in "The Storm." In "Désirée's Baby," water also plays an important part in the plot, as she walks into the bayou with her baby son, presumably to disappear there with her child. Water represents a complex combination of true freedom and the vast, unknown beyond, and students may have different interpretations of what the significance of water is in Chopin's writing, depending on what stories and examples they choose.

Strong responses should include a close reading of at least 1-2 different examples of water being incorporated into the selected stories, employing direct textual evidence and original analysis of the importance of the similarities and differences between the use of these themes in the scenes or examples being examined. In addition, the strongest responses will include an examination of how Chopin's writing on these themes changes over the course of her works. Although there are other strong ways to approach this essay question, a particularly good approach would include selecting one of the earlier references to water and comparing and contrasting it to later examples for analysis, examining how the two different scenes take different approaches to these symbols and reflect different meanings. Finally, the strongest answers will examine and evaluate the implications and, if applicable, possible causes of any shifts in perspective that have taken place between the two (or more) scenes/examples.

Final Exam

Multiple Choice

Circle the letter corresponding to the best answer.

1. Where was Kate Chopin (née O'Flaherty) originally from?

    A. New Orleans
    B. Atlanta
    C. New York
    D. St. Louis

2. What was the name of Kate Chopin's first novel?

    A. "At Fault"
    B. "An Honorable Woman"
    C. "The Sea"
    D. "The Awakening"

3. Which is NOT one of the settings where events take place in "The Awakening"?

    A. Grand Isle
    B. New Orleans
    C. Biloxi
    D. Chênière

4. Who owns the estate that includes the summer cottages at which the Pontelliers stay in "The Awakening"?

    A. The Lebrun Family
    B. The Ratignolle Family
    C. The Pontellier Family
    D. The Reisz Family

5. With whom does Edna Pontellier share NOT share any flirtations?

A. Monsieur Robert Lebrun
B. Monsieur Ratignolle
C. Monsieur Arobin
D. Monsieur Victor Lebrun

6. Where does Robert go when he leaves Grand Isle to do business?

A. New Orleans
B. New York
C. Mexico
D. Atlanta

7. At the end of "The Awakening," how does Edna decide to take her own life?

A. By poisoning herself in one of the cabins at Grand Isle
B. By swimming into the ocean until she grows too weary to continue
C. By walking out into the dark and remote bayou near Grand Isle in the middle of the night
D. By throwing herself in front of of a cable car in New Orleans

8. To what woman does Léonce Pontellier unfavorably compare his own wife's womanly and motherly qualities early on in "The Awakening"?

A. Madame Ratignolle
B. Mademoiselle Reisz
C. Mrs. Highcamp
D. Madame Lebrun

9. Who is Athénaïse's husband?

A. Léonce
B. Armand
C. Monteclin
D. Cazeau

10. Where does Athénaïse's husband go to look for her initially?

A. The secret apartment she's been keeping behind her husband's back
B. Her parent's home
C. Her brother's house
D. A boarding-house in New Orleans

11. Why does Gouvernail say he wants to come stay with the Barodas at their plantation for a few weeks?

A. He says he wants to come hunt with Mr. Baroda, but is secretly carrying on an illicit affair with Mrs. Baroda
B. His marriage has just dissolved and he needs to be with Mr. Baroda, an old friend
C. He needs to get away from the city for health reasons
D. He wants to relax and have some peace from his normally-hectic city life

12. Why does Mrs. Baroda originally not want Gouvernail to come visit the Baroda's estate for a few weeks?

A. The house was having repairs done and it isn't in a suitable state for guests.
B. She has met Gouvernail before and does not like him.
C. Mrs. Baroda is tired from a hectic winter of socializing and wanted some one-on-one time with her husband.
D. She and Mr. Baroda were having marital problems and she did not want anyone there to witness their arguments.

13. What word does Louise Mallard keep repeating over and over to herself in "The Story of an Hour"?

A. Accident
B. Joy
C. Free
D. Love

14. How does Louise Mallard find out her husband is still alive?

A. Louise sees him walking up to the house through her bedroom window
B. A courier arrives to announce that the newspaper had been misprinted

C. He walks in the door, surprising everyone

D. Her husband's friend, Richards, tells Louise that Brently is actually alive

15. What is the name of Calixta's old boyfriend in "The Storm"?

A. Alcée

B. Robert

C. Gouvernail

D. Bobinôt

16. Why does Calixta's old boyfriend end up coming inside her house?

A. The storm is getting worse and worse and he must take shelter

B. He is thirsty and she offers him a drink

C. His horse is injured and he needs to wait for help

D. He wants to visit with Bobinôt and plans to wait for him there

17. Where did Désirée, the protagonist of "Désirée's Baby," come from originally?

A. She is an escaped slave and is trying to pass as a white woman in New Orleans

B. She was abandoned at the gates of the Valmondé estate

C. She is the biological daughter of the Valmondés

D. She is the secret daughter of Monsieur Valmondé and one of his mistresses

18. What does Armand do with Désirée's belongings when he tells her to leave the estate?

A. He burns them on a bonfire

B. He returns them to the Valmondé estate

C. He dumps them in the ocean

D. He makes Désirée carry all of her belongings with her when she leaves

19. In "A Pair of Silk Stockings," how much money does Mrs. Sommers find herself unexpectedly in possession of?

A. Fifty dollars

B. Two dollars

C. Two hundred dollars

D. Fifteen dollars

20. What happens that suddenly makes Mrs. Sommers want to go shopping for herself?

A. She decides to treat herself to a nice lunch and drinks wine, which makes her less disciplined than usual

B. She has an argument with her husband which makes her want to spend the money imprudently

C. She is tempted by the feel of a pair of silk stockings

D. She sees a pair of silk stockings that she's always coveted and abandons all ofher practical plans

Short Answer

1. What event in Kate Chopin's life caused her to leave her married home in New Orleans to go back to her home city?

   _____

2. What was the critical reception when "The Awakening" was originally published?

   _____

3. In "The Awakening," what two forms of cathartic release does Edna's relationship with Mademoiselle Reisz provide her with?

   _____

4. Where does Edna Pontellier move when she decides to leave the big Pontellier house on Esplanade Street?

   _____

5. In "The Story of an Hour," why can't Louise Mallard be told of her husband's death in a direct and up-front manner?

   _____

6. In the story bearing her name, what sort of husband is Cazeau to his wife, Athénaïse?

   _____

7. In "A Respectable Woman," what quality attracts Mrs. Baroda to Gouvernail?

   _____

8. In "Désirée's Baby," what experience makes Désirée realize the truth about her baby's heritage?

_____

9. In "The Storm," where are Calixta's husband and son stuck as the torrent blows through?

_____

10. In "A Pair of Silk Stockings," what items does Mrs. Sommers initially consider purchasing with her money?

_____

Vocabulary Questions

Terms

1. _____ incessantly
2. _____ toothsome
3. _____ commodious
4. _____ grotesque
5. _____ imploring
6. _____ languishing
7. _____ baneful
8. _____ paramount
9. _____ inviolate
10. _____ suffused

Answers

A. begging, requesting earnestly or desperately
B. destructive or harmful
C. becoming feeble, weak, or lacking liveliness
D. vital, supremely important
E. covered, permeated, bathed
F. luscious, delicious, mouthwatering
G. constantly, unceasingly, continually
H. spacious, roomy, comfortable
I. twisted, distorted, bizarre (sometimes comically so)
J. safe from violation, untouchable

Short Essays

1. In *The Awakening*, what is the purpose of the childbirth scene with Madame Ratignolle? What does the scene demonstrate about Adèle? Edna?

_____

_____

_____

_____

_____

2. How do you interpret the ending of "The Story of an Hour"?

_____

_____

_____

_____

_____

3. What do you think Chopin intends to convey about race relations during her era in the way she ends "Désirée's Baby"?

_____

_____

_____

_____

_____

Final Exam Answer Key

Multiple Choice

1. **(D)** St. Louis
2. **(A)** "At Fault"
3. **(C)** Biloxi
4. **(A)** The Lebrun Family
5. **(B)** Monsieur Ratignolle
6. **(C)** Mexico
7. **(B)** By swimming into the ocean until she grows too weary to continue
8. **(A)** Madame Ratignolle
9. **(D)** Cazeau
10. **(B)** Her parent's home
11. **(D)** He wants to relax and have some peace from his normally-hectic city life
12. **(C)** Mrs. Baroda is tired from a hectic winter of socializing and wanted some one-on-one time with her husband.
13. **(C)** Free
14. **(C)** He walks in the door, surprising everyone
15. **(A)** Alcée
16. **(A)** The storm is getting worse and worse and he must take shelter
17. **(B)** She was abandoned at the gates of the Valmondé estate
18. **(A)** He burns them on a bonfire
19. **(D)** Fifteen dollars
20. **(C)** She is tempted by the feel of a pair of silk stockings

Short Answer

1. Chopin became a widow in 1883 when her husband died of swamp fever. She managed her husband's business for a year but then moved back to St. Louis
2. "The Awakening" inspired a storm of controversy for what was considered at the time to be an unprecedented and scandalous representation of female sexuality, marriage, and motherhood.
3. Edna's relationship with Mademoiselle Reisz is a complex one, but it includes opportunities to connect to her emotions through evocative music and to feel a connection with Robert since Mademoiselle receives letters from him.
4. Edna moves to a small, cozy house around the corner from her family's home, which some start referring to as the "pigeon house."
5. Mrs. Mallard has a heart condition that can be exacerbated by stress.

6. Although it seems at first like Cazeau may not be a good husband, since Athénaïse wants to get out of the marriage, it turns out he actually is a good, loving, patient husband.
7. Gouvernail's voice and his sudden willingness to talk about himself both intrigue and attract Mrs. Baroda to him.
8. One day, as Désirée watches her son play, she glances at one of the mixed-race slave children and sees the striking resemblance.
9. They get stuck at Freidheimer's, a grocery store.
10. After thinking about it, Mrs. Sommers decides to spend a bit more on Janie's shoes so they will last longer, to purchase some cloth to make her children new garments, and to get everyone new hats and stockings.

Vocabulary Questions

1. G incessantly: constantly, unceasingly, continually
2. F toothsome: luscious, delicious, mouthwatering
3. H commodious: spacious, roomy, comfortable
4. I grotesque: twisted, distorted, bizarre (sometimes comically so)
5. A imploring: begging, requesting earnestly or desperately
6. C languishing: becoming feeble, weak, or lacking liveliness
7. B baneful: destructive or harmful
8. D paramount: vital, supremely important
9. J inviolate: safe from violation, untouchable
10. E suffused: covered, permeated, bathed

Short Essays

1. In this scene, the reader sees Madame Ratignolle in a starkly different light than she's ever appeared before. Whereas Chopin has, up until this point, portrayed Madame Ratignolle as a perfect traditional New Orleans Creole wife and mother, with Madonna-like beauty and a kind, ever-patient temperament. In this scene, however, Madame Ratignolle is in tremendous pain, at the height of childbirth, and therefore looks unattractive and full of venom and rage towards those who are trying to help her. In addition, her hair is braided down and lies "coiled like a golden serpent" on the sofa beside her. Some students might note that this metaphor evokes biblical symbolism, representing the serpent tempting Adam and Eve in the Garden of Eden. In this moment, Madame Ratignolle shows the dark side of the human condition, revealing it to be full of pain and turmoil, even with the comforts afforded to the social elite. In addition, Madame Ratignolle's inability to maintain her motherly serenity in this torturous moment reveals to Edna the futility of romanticizing life and the world. Edna is also reminded of the pain of her own childbirths and relives the painful ordeal, leaving her feeling "stunned and speechless with emotion."

More broadly, this entire passage does something that was very unusual for the time -- it portrays the pain of childbirth in an unromantic, stark, and unforgiving light. In so doing, this passage undermines the beautiful serenity so prized in the cult of motherhood that was a prevalent part of the culture in Chopin's time. This scene confronts the reader with the true, raw, painful process of childbirth, stripping even the most admirable of mothers (Madame Ratignolle) of all of the characteristics normally associated with motherhood, simply showing her as she experiences pain like any other person. By giving the reader a window into the pain of childbirth -- arguably the time when a woman is in her most maternal state -- Chopin suggests the ridiculousness of defining women's value only by their ability to give birth to children and be good mothers.

2. This question is very open-ended, so students could come to the table with all sorts of different opinions and approaches. Student answers should first demonstrate an understanding of the important facets of the ending of the story. As a review, after learning that her husband has died in a train accident, Louise Mallard was initially incredibly distraught, but then realizes she is now free to lead her life how she chooses and is excited. Suddenly, the front door opens, and Brently Mallard (Louise's husband) walks in. He is slightly disheveled from his trip, but hasn't been killed in a train accident and didn't even know one took place. Josephine (Louise's sister) shrieks as Richards (Brently's friend) tries to block Louise from the shock of seeing her husband, who she'd just been told was dead, suddenly come back to life. But he is too late. When doctors arrive, they say Louise died of a heart attack brought on by joy.

Some students might think that she is so overwhelmed by joy because she has learned of her freedom. Others might think that Louise's heart gave out to save her from the idea that she would have to return to her life as a wife. Still others may argue that her husband's *return* is what brings on her tremendous joy, and that she was deluding herself into thinking she was happy about his death. Encourage students to find textual evidence (words, phrases, other parts of the story, etc.) to support their perspectives, since this question is so open-ended.

3. As part of this essay topic, students should demonstrate an understanding of the important elements of the ending of the story. Although the reader does not actually get to see Armand's reaction to his recent discovery that he is, in fact, the one who has a mixed-race heritage. Because of Armand's incredibly cold and cruel reaction to Désirée, it is clear that he was shocked and ashamed to learn that he might have married a woman who was half-black -- this would have been a typical response for the time period. The fact that Chopin decides to turn the tables on Armand at the end of the story suggests that the author is trying to make a point about how muddied and complicated racial histories actually are and point out the hypocrisies of the culture in which she lived.

Lesson Plans

Gr▲deSaver™
Getting you the grade since 1999™

Other Lesson Plans from GradeSaver™

12 Angry Men
1984
A Christmas Carol
A Confederacy of
   Dunces
A Doll's House
A Farewell to Arms
Alexander Hamilton
Alice in Wonderland
Allen Ginsberg's
   Poetry
All Quiet on the
   Western Front
All the Light We
   Cannot See
Americanah
Angela's Ashes
Animal Farm
An Inspector Calls
Anna Karenina
Antigone
A Passage to India
A Raisin in the Sun

Arcadia
A Room With a
   View
Around the World in
   80 Days
A Separate Peace
As I Lay Dying
A Streetcar Named
   Desire
A Tale of Two Cities
A Thousand
   Splendid Suns
Atonement
A View From the
   Bridge
Beloved
Beowulf
Between the World
   and Me
Bhagavad-Gita
Black Boy
Bless Me, Ultima
Brave New World

Breakfast at
   Tiffany's
Bury My Heart at
   Wounded Knee
Call of the Wild
Cane
Cannery Row
Catching Fire
Cathedral
Cat's Cradle
Ceremony
Christopher
   Marlowe's Poems
Connecticut Yankee
   in King Arthur's
   Court
Death of a Salesman
Desire Under the
   Elms
Do Androids Dream
   of Electric Sheep?
Doctor Faustus
   (Marlowe)

For our full list of over 300 Study Guides, Quizzes, Lesson Plans
Sample College Application Essays, Literature Essays and E-texts, visit:

www.gradesaver.com

Lesson Plans

GradeSaver™
Getting you the grade since 1999™

Other Lesson Plans from GradeSaver™

Don Quixote Book I
Dr. Jekyll and Mr.
  Hyde
Dubliners
Emily Dickinson's
  Collected Poems
Emma
Ender's Game
Equus
Esperanza Rising
Everyman: Morality
  Play
Fahrenheit 451
Fangirl
Fear and Loathing in
  Las Vegas
Flannery O'Connor's
  Stories
Flowers for
  Algernon
For Colored Girls
  Who Have
  Considered

Suicide When the
  Rainbow Is Enuf
Founding Brothers
Frankenstein
Franny and Zooey
Gone Girl
Go Set a Watchman
Go Tell it On the
  Mountain
Great Expectations
Green Grass,
  Running Water
Gulliver's Travels
Hamlet
Hatchet
Heart of Darkness
Holes
Homegoing
House of Mirth
House on Mango
  Street

How the Garcia
  Girls Lost Their
  Accents
I Am Malala
I Know Why the
  Caged Bird Sings
Incidents in the Life
  of a Slave Girl
In Cold Blood
In the Penal Colony
In the Time of the
  Butterflies
Into the Wild
Into Thin Air
Invisible Man
Island of the Blue
  Dolphins
Jane Eyre
John Donne: Poems
Jorge Borges: Short
  Stories

For our full list of over 300 Study Guides, Quizzes, Lesson Plans
Sample College Application Essays, Literature Essays and E-texts, visit:

www.gradesaver.com

Lesson Plans

GradeSaver™

Getting you the grade since 1999™

Other Lesson Plans from GradeSaver™

Journey to the
  Center of the
  Earth
Julius Caesar
July's People
Juno and the
  Paycock
Kate Chopin's Short
  Stories
Kindred
King Lear
Last of the
  Mohicans
Leaves of Grass
Let the Circle be
  Unbroken
Life of Pi
Little Women
Looking for Alaska
Lord Byron's Poems
Lord Jim
Lord of the Flies
Macbeth

Master Harold...
  And the Boys
MAUS
Medea
Merchant of Venice
Middlemarch
Middlesex
Mockingjay
Montana 1948
Mother Courage and
  Her Children
Mrs. Dalloway
My Antonia
My Brilliant Friend
My Children! My
  Africa!
Mythology
Native Son
Never Let Me Go
Night
Number the Stars
Oedipus Rex or
  Oedipus the King

Of Mice and Men
Oliver Twist
One Flew Over the
  Cuckoo's Nest
One Hundred Years
  of Solitude
O Pioneers
Oroonoko
Oryx and Crake
Othello
Our Town
Paper Towns
Percy Shelley:
  Poems
Persepolis: The
  Story of a
  Childhood
Poe's Poetry
Portrait of the Artist
  as a Young Man
Pride and Prejudice
Purple Hibiscus
Pygmalion

For our full list of over 300 Study Guides, Quizzes, Lesson Plans
Sample College Application Essays, Literature Essays and E-texts, visit:

www.gradesaver.com

Lesson Plans

GradeSaver™

Getting you the grade since 1999™

Other Lesson Plans from GradeSaver™

Reading Lolita in Tehran

Rhinoceros

Rip Van Winkle and Other Stories

Robert Frost: Poems

Robinson Crusoe

Roll of Thunder, Hear My Cry

Romeo and Juliet

Roots

Rosencrantz and Guildenstern Are Dead

Shakespeare's Sonnets

Short Stories of Ernest Hemingway

Siddhartha

Snow Country

Songs of Innocence and of Experience

Speak

Spring Awakening

Station Eleven

Sula

Tender is the Night

Tess of the D'Urbervilles

The Absolutely True Diary of a Part-Time Indian

The Adventures of Huckleberry Finn

The Adventures of Tom Sawyer

The Alchemist (Coelho)

The American

The Autobiography of Benjamin Franklin

The Awakening

The Bell Jar

The Bloody Chamber

The Book Thief

The Boy in the Striped Pajamas

The Brief Wondrous Life of Oscar Wao

The Canterbury Tales

The Catcher in the Rye

The Cherry Orchard

The Chosen

The Color Purple

The Count of Monte Cristo

The Crucible

The Curious Incident of the Dog in the Night-time

The Death of Ivan Ilych

For our full list of over 300 Study Guides, Quizzes, Lesson Plans
Sample College Application Essays, Literature Essays and E-texts, visit:

www.gradesaver.com

Lesson Plans

GradeSaver™
Getting you the grade since 1999™

Other Lesson Plans from GradeSaver™

The Moonlit Road and Other Ghost and Horror Stories

The Namesake

The Necklace

The Odyssey

The Old Man and the Sea

The Once and Future King

The Outsiders

The Overcoat

The Pearl

The Perks of Being a Wallflower

The Phantom of the Opera

The Phantom Tollbooth

The Poisonwood Bible

The Quiet American

The Red Badge of Courage

The Rime of the Ancient Mariner

The Road

The Scarlet Letter

The Seagull

The Secret Life of Bees

The Story of My Life

The Stranger

The Tempest

The Things They Carried

The Tortilla Curtain

The Turn of the Screw

The Waste Land

The Wave

The Westing Game

The Woman Warrior

The Wonderful Wizard of Oz

The Yellow Wallpaper

Things Fall Apart

Thirteen Reasons Why

To Build a Fire

To Kill a Mockingbird

Topdog/Underdog

Top Girls

To the Lighthouse

Touching Spirit Bear

Trifles

Uncle Tom's Cabin

Waiting for Godot

Waiting for Lefty

Walden

Washington Square

Watership Down

Weep Not, Child

GrAdeSaver™

Getting you the grade since 1999™

Other Lesson Plans from GradeSaver™

We Need New
Names

Where the Red Fern
Grows

White Teeth

Wide Sargasso Sea

Wonder

Wordsworth's
Poetical Works

Wuthering Heights

Young Goodman
Brown and Other
Hawthorne Short
Stories

For our full list of over 300 Study Guides, Quizzes, Lesson Plans
Sample College Application Essays, Literature Essays and E-texts, visit:

www.gradesaver.com

Made in the USA
Lexington, KY
11 August 2019